Diet recommendations for acquired lactose intolerance

Please check these recommendations always with a nutrition consultant, therapist, doctor or dietician. The recipes and the list of ingredients are supporting the conventional medical therapy.
The calorie disclosures of fresh ingredients (fruit and vegetables) vary according to quality and time of harvest. The contents were checked by a dietician and a nutrition consultant for the Traditional Chinese Medicine (TCM).

Author:
©2017 Josef Miligui
www.ebns.at

Source:
The lists are created from the EBNS database for nutritional counseling. The database is used by dietitians, therapists and doctors for advising the patient / client.

Literature:
The specialist literature and the training documents of the German and Austrian dietary and traditional Chinese medicine serve as a knowledge base. We have used the documents as a basis of knowledge, adapted it to our experience and completed them.
http://di-book.com

Title Photo:
©2008 Erika Weixlbaumer

Production and publishing:
BoD – Books on Demand, Norderstedt
ISBN: 9783752803952

Diet recommendations for DIETETICS - Gastrointestinal tract - Small intestine and large intestine - Acquired lactose intolerance (lactose malabsorption)

1 Treatment strategy

The principle of nutritional therapy consists in the restriction or renunciation of the consumption of milk and products as well as of foods containing them.

Although sour milk products (yoghurt, milk, kefir, etc.) contain relatively large amounts of milk sugar, they are often well tolerated. The reason for this are the lactic acid bacteria which decompose larger quantities of milk sugar. They are better tolerated if they are already older and the bacteria already had more time to break the milk sugar.

The same applies to the compatibility of many cheese varieties, since milk sugar is largely degraded during the production of cheese by fermentation.

It is important for the nutritional practice when the milk of sour milk and cheese can be consumed, as at least a part of the calcium requirement is thereby covered.

In addition, sour milk products ensure a well-functioning intestinal flora.

As a substitute for conventional milk and dairy products, lactose-free products can be chosen (here the sugar has already been split) or soy, rice and oat milk products.

Sheep, goat and mares also contain lactose.

Lactose may also be present as a binder in sausages, finished products and medicaments.

2 Avoid

Milk / dairy products, cheese *, dried milk, pudding, mixed drinks, cocoa, desserts, coffee whites, condensed milk, cream, sour cream, fat milk *, kefir *, yoghurt *, sour milk *, whey *, curd cheese.

Bread / pastry with milk,

Milk powder could be contained in: Bread- u. Cakes, biscuits, crispbread, crackers.

Ready-to-serve: Pizza, frozen pastry, canned, meat or vegetable preparations.

Sweets: ice cream, chocolate, cream and caramel sweets, sweet bars, nougat, nut nougat cream, chocolates.

Meat / sausage products: sausages (for example, sausages), liver sausage, fat reduced sausage products, sausage preserves.

Instant products: instant soups, instant sauces, instant creams, mashed potato powder, dumpling powder, brioche mixes.

Finished sauces: gourmet sauces, grilled sauces, salad dressing, mayonnaise.

Other products: muesli mixtures, margarine products, coating creams.

* The marked foods contain different amounts of lactose.

3 Breakfast

4 Snack

5 Lunch

6 Afternoon

7 Dinner

8   Any time

9 Recipes

(recommendable) = You can use more.
(little) = You should use less than specified or omit.

9.1 8 treasures of rice

Diuretic, warming the body from the inside, expands blood vessels, strengthens the muscles, regulates internal organs functions, promotes spleen, calms nerves.
Cooking time approx. 1 hour
Calories p. portion: 212
4 portions
Allergens:

Quantity of ingredients:
Lily bulbs 1 table spoon / 5g. (recommended)
Longane 1 table spoon / 5g. (yes)
King Solomon's-seal 1 table spoon / 5g. (yes)
Yam root, yam root tuber 1 table spoon / 5g. (yes)
Coix (seeds) YiYi Ren 1 table spoon / 5g. (yes)
Rice wild (nature rice) 1 1/2 cups / 240g. (recommended)
Water 8-10 cups / 800g. (yes)

Cooking instructions:
Each one 1 tbsp:
Bai He, Longan, Yu Zhu, Da Zao, Shan Yao, Lian Mi, Yi Yi Ren, Qian Shi
Add hot water and soak for about 30 minutes. Then add 1 - 2 cups of rice (normal) and simmer for 1/2 to 1 hour until the rice is very soft. Or: Cook for about 3 hours with the herbs a congee. Then the herbs do not have to be soaked.

9.2 Andalusian fish pot

Strengthens immune system, prevents cancer, dissolves stagnation, promotes weight loss. Good to fight immunodeficiency, loss of appetite, flatulence, high blood pressure, depressions, diabetes, diarrhea, stimulates appetite.
Cooking time approx. 30 min
Calories p. portion: 348
4 portions
Allergens: ADLO

Quantity of ingredients:
Basic recipe for a vegetable soup (nutritious) 2 cups / 500g. (yes)
Onion (spring onion) 2 pieces / 40g. (yes)
Olive oil 1 table spoon / 20g. (yes)
Lemon peel 1/2 piece / 3g. (yes)
Bay leaf 1 piece / 1g. (yes)
Potato 5/8 oz / 200g. (yes)
Cod 3/4 lbs / 300g. (recommended)
White wine 4 table spoons / 80g. (little)
Lemon juice 1/2 teaspoon / 10g. (yes)
Salt 1 pinch / 1g. (little)
Pepper (ground) 1 pinch / 0,2g. (yes)
Parsley 1 table spoon / 15g. (yes)
White bread (wheat bread) 8 slices / 250g. (little)

Cooking instructions:
Boil the vegetable broth with small spring onion, olive oil, grated lemon peel and bay leaf. Boil covered for 10 minutes. Add the peeled, diced potatoes and boil in about 8 minutes. Add fish pieces and white wine and switch to small heat. In the slightly boiling broth put the fish and boil it a few minutes. Season with lemon juice, salt and pepper. Serve with parsley sprinkled.
White bread as a side dish.

9.3   Asparagus with lemon pesto

Diuretic, improves blood circulation, prevents cancer, forcing spleen, promotes weight loss. Good to fight immunodeficiency, loss of appetite, arteriosclerosis, flatulence, bladder weakness, anemia, high blood pressure, depressions, diabetes, diarrhea, vomiting.
Cooking time approx. 20 min
Calories p. portion: 172
2 portions
Allergens: H

Quantity of ingredients:
Asparagus (green or white) 1,1 lbs / 500g. (recommended)
Lemon 1 piece / 35g. (yes)
Water hot 1/2 cup / 50g. (yes)
Boxhorn clover seeds 1 pinch / 0,2g. (yes)
Olive oil 2 table spoons / 20g. (yes)
Almond 1 table spoon / 8g. (yes)
Sugar cane sugar 1 pinch / 0,5g. (little)

Garlic 1 clove / 2g. (yes)
Pepper (ground) 1 pinch / 0,2g. (yes)
Salt 1 pinch / 0,5g. (little)

Cooking instructions:
Peel the asparagus (the whites whole, the greens only at the bottom). Peel and cut diagonally into pieces about 3 cm long. In the steam sieve the white about 12 minutes, the green about 10 minutes to cook. Cut the lemon into small pieces, remove seeds. Add the remaining ingredients and puree to a creamy sauce. Arrange the asparagus and cover with the lemon pesto.
This fits rice, bulgur or millet.

9.4   Avocado with lemon

Good to fight insomnia, inflammation, swelling, pain and itching. Is calming.
Cooking time approx. 5 min
Calories p. portion: 289
1 portions
Allergens:

Quantity of ingredients:
Avocado 1/2 piece / 120g. (yes)
Lemon juice 1/2 piece / 10g. (yes)
Salt 1 pinch / 1g. (little)

Cooking instructions:
Halve the avocado, remove the core, add the lemon juice, salt a little and eat with a spoon.

9.5   Banana Soymilk

Good to fight loss of appetite, oral mucosa inflammation. Strengthens body energy, promotes stomach-spleen harmony, promotes digestion, regulates gastrointestinal function. Relieves pain, detoxifying, bactericide.
Cooking time approx. 5 min
Calories p. portion: 126
2 portions
Allergens: E

Quantity of ingredients:
Banana 1 piece / 120g. (yes)
Soybean milk 1 1/2 cups / 400g. (yes)
Honey 1 teaspoon / 3g. (yes)
Cinnamon ground 1 pinch / 1g. (yes)
Acerola fruit nectar or powder 1 teaspoon / 2g. (yes)

Cooking instructions:
Cut the banana into pieces, puree them with soy milk, acerola, honey
and cinnamon with the mixing stick.

9.6   Barley mash with steamed pear

Promotes digestion, supports urination, promotes spleen, diuretic,
forcing spleen, relaxes, promotes perspiration.
Cooking time approx. 25 min
Calories p. portion: 114
5 portions
Allergens: A

Quantity of ingredients:
Water 10 cups / 1200g. (yes)
Barley 1 cup / 120g. (yes)
Ginger fresh 2 slices / 2g. (yes)
Cardamom 3 capsules / 1g. (yes)
Salt 1 pinch / 1g. (little)
Pear 1 piece / 200g. (recommended)
Sugar cane sugar 1/2 teaspoon / 5g. (little)

Cooking instructions:
Grind coarse the barley and roast it dry. Add hot water, add ginger and
cardamom and let it swell to a pulp in low heat. Peel and dice the pear
and boil for 10 minutes with a little water. At the end, add the stewed
pear, a little butter and sweetener.

Variant: If you want to go fast, you can use barley flakes instead of shot.

9.7 Basic recipe for a beef broth (clear)

Strengthens muscles, tendons and bones, reduces blood pressure, strengthens immune system, prevents cancer, reduces radiation damage, stimulates digestion, reduces pain, promotes digestion, diuretic. Rosemary stimulates digestion.
Cooking time approx. 4-8 hours
Calories p. portion: 114
10 portions
Allergens: O

Quantity of ingredients:
Beef soup meat 1,1 lbs / 500g. (yes)
Beef meatbones 5/8 oz / 200g. (yes)
Vinegar (Red wine vinegar) 1 dash / 3g. (yes)
Juniper berry 8 pieces / 6g. (recommended)
Rosemary 1 pinch / 1g. (yes)
Carrot 3 pieces / 210g. (recommended)
Parsnip 2 pieces / 300g. (yes)
Leek 1 piece / 200g. (yes)
Ginger fresh 1/2 teaspoon / 5g. (yes)
Lovage 1 stem / 15g. (yes)
Clove 2 pieces / 2g. (yes)
Pimento 6 pieces / 12g. (yes)
Anise (Common Fennel) 2 pieces / 1g. (yes)
Salt 1 teaspoon / 5g. (little)
Water 3,3 lbs / 1300g. (yes)

Cooking instructions:
Heat water, a dash of red wine vinegar, some juniper berries, a little rosemary, bones and meat till it boils; add carrot, parsnip, leek, ginger, lovage, clove, allspice, star anise and a little salt; simmer for 4-8 hours then strain.
Refrigerate for later use.

9.8 Basic recipe for a chicken broth worming

Strengthens blood, strengthens bone marrow, reduces blood pressure, strengthens immune system, prevents cancer, reduces radiation damage, promotes sweating, dissolves stagnation, good to fight loss of appetite, flatulence.
Cooking time approx. 2-3 hours
Calories p. portion: 90
9 portions

Allergens: L

Quantity of ingredients:
Chicken meat 1/2 piece / 600g. (yes)
Carrot 2 pieces / 150g. (recommended)
Leek 1 stick / 45g. (yes)
Celery root 1 piece / 500g. (recommended)
Ginger fresh 2 slices / 2g. (yes)
Fenugreek (Trigonella foenum-graecum) 1 teaspoon / 2g. (yes)
Juniper berry 1 teaspoon / 3g. (recommended)
Bay leaf 3 pieces / 2g. (yes)
Water 4 cup / 900g. (yes)

Cooking instructions:
Remove chicken parts from fat. Place chicken pieces in a saucepan
with hot water and heat till it boils briefly, skimming any resulting foam.
Add coarsely chopped vegetables and all spices and cook over medium
heat for 2 to 3 hours. Strain the finished soup. Throw away vegetables
and bones.
Tip: If you want to use the meat as a soup insert, take out after 45
minutes and return only the bones in the soup.
Refrigerate for later use.

9.9   Basic recipe for a duck broth

Forcing spleen, strengthens blood, supports urination, reduces blood
pressure, strengthens immune system, prevents cancer, reduces
radiation damage.
Cooking time approx. 2-3 hours
Calories p. portion: 61
6 portions
Allergens: L

Quantity of ingredients:
Duck (heart) 5/8 oz / 200g. (yes)
Water 2 cup / 450g. (yes)
Duck (slaughtered) 1/4 lbs - 4oz / 100g. (yes)
Carrot 2 pieces / 100g. (recommended)
Celery root 1/2 piece / 600g. (recommended)

Cooking instructions:
Cook duck pieces with vegetables for 2-3 hours. Sift broth through a
fine sieve and refrigerate for later use.

The innards can be reused: You cut them finely and leaves them for a few minutes with fresh vegetables in the broth draw. Sprinkle with parsley before serving.

9.10 Basic recipe for a fish broth

Strengthens the kidneys, promotes watering, reduces blood pressure, strengthens immune system, prevents cancer, reduces radiation damage. Low in cholesterol and protein rich. Improves blood circulation, stimulates appetite.
Cooking time approx. 40 min
Calories p. portion: 128
5 portions
Allergens: DLO

Quantity of ingredients:
Fish pieces mixed (fresh water) 3/4 lbs / 300g. (recommended)
Celery root 1/4 lbs - 4oz / 120g. (recommended)
Leek 2 inches / 10g. (yes)
Carrot 2 pieces / 150g. (recommended)
White wine 1/2 cup / 125g. (little)
Lemon 1/2 piece / 50g. (yes)
Bay leaf 2 leaves / 2g. (yes)
Peppercorns 3 pieces / 2g. (yes)
Olive oil 1 table spoon / 10g. (yes)
Water 2 cup / 450g. (yes)

Cooking instructions:
Fry celery, chopped carrots and leeks in olive oil, add bay leaf and peppercorns, add pieces of fish and sauté briefly. Add water, add little white wine or lemon. Simmer gently for 30 minutes. Skim off the resulting foam several times. In the end, sift the ingredients through a cloth.
Refrigerate for later use

9.11 Basic recipe for a reissue soup (Congee)

Low fat content, for the drainage of the body overweight and high blood pressure.
Cooking time approx. 2-4 hours
Calories p. portion: 140
3 portions
Allergens:

Quantity of ingredients:
Rice variety any 1 cup / 120g. (yes)
Water 6 cups / 700g. (yes)

Cooking instructions:
Cook rice and water in a ratio of about 1: 6. The amount of water determines the thickness of the mash (matter of taste).
Put the rice in a saucepan with a heavy lid. It is important to simmer the rice after a short boil on the slightest flame, otherwise it burns.
Boil the rice for 2-4 hours. The longer he cooks, the more he strengthens.
If you want to eat the dish for breakfast, you can put the rice on just before bedtime.
To be on the safe side, you should first check the behavior of your pot and cooker under observation for a similar amount of time, so that nothing burns. Refrigerate for later use.

9.12 Basic recipe for a vegetable soup, nutritious

Reduces blood pressure, strengthens immune system, prevents cancer, forcing spleen, dissolves stagnation, promotes weight loss. Good to fight immunodeficiency, high blood pressure, depressions, diabetes, diarrhea, reduces blood lipids.
Cooking time approx. 2-3 hours
Calories p. portion: 48
5 portions
Allergens: L

Quantity of ingredients:
Olive oil 1 table spoon / 4g. (yes)
Onion white 1 piece / 60g. (yes)
Carrot 3 pieces / 200g. (recommended)
Parsnip 3/8 lbs - 6oz / 150g. (yes)
Celery root 1 cup / 100g. (recommended)
Ginger fresh 1/2 teaspoon / 2g. (yes)
Lemon 1/2 piece / 25g. (yes)
Juniper berry 6 pieces / 6g. (recommended)
Thyme dried 1 pinch / 1g. (yes)
Lovage 1 table spoon / 3g. (yes)
Bay leaf 2 leaves / 1g. (yes)
Salt 1 pinch / 1g. (little)
Water 3 cups / 650g. (yes)

Cooking instructions:
Cut the vegetables into cubes.
Heat oil in hot pot, fry shortly onions and vegetables.
Add cold water, then add ginger, bay leaf and lemon juice.
Season with juniper, thyme and lovage. Cover for 2 - 3 hours on a low heat and simmer.
The used vegetables should be thrown away.
The basic recipe serves as a soup base and to refine vegetables, legumes or cereals.
If you want to eat vegetable soup immediately, add the desired vegetables half an hour before.
Refrigerate for later use.

9.13 Beef broth

Warming and nourishing, forces.
Cooking time approx. 2-6 hours
Calories p. portion: 125
7 portions
Allergens: L

Quantity of ingredients:
Water 4 cup / 1000g. (yes)
Lemon 2 daches / 2g. (yes)
Beef meat 1,1 lbs / 500g. (yes)
Beef meatbones 2 pieces / 0g. (yes)
Turmeric (yellow root) 1 pinch / 1g. (yes)
Carrot 2 pieces / 100g. (recommended)
Celery root 1 inch / 25g. (recommended)
Parsley root 1 piece / 150g. (yes)
Onion white 1 piece / 50g. (yes)
Bay leaf 2-3 leaves / 2g. (yes)
Coriander 1/2 teaspoon / 2g. (yes)
Ginger fresh 1 inch / 2g. (yes)
Wakame 1 inch / 1g. (yes)
Parsley 1 stem / 10g. (yes)

Cooking instructions:
In a saucepan with water (enough to cover the meat), add a few drops of lemon juice, a little turmeric, beef and bones, heat till it boils and simmer for a while; then pour away the whole broth, clean the pot, rinse off meat and bones with hot water (this will save you from foaming) and

put it back to the saucepan with hot water (amount as you like); add a good pinch of turmeric, carrot, celery, parsley root to the pot; add onion, bay leaves, coriander, a piece of sliced ginger, a strip of wakame, a stalk of parsley; boil everything together and simmer for 2-6 hours (if the meat is to be used otherwise, take it out of the broth after 1 1/2 - 2 hours, as soon as it is cooked, the bones are returned to the broth); When the cooking time is over, pour the broth through a sieve and discard all ingredients.

Notes: The longer the broth has cooked, the warmer but more nourishing it is. It is after cooling for 3-4 days in the refrigerator durable. The broth can be drunk hot or used as a base for soups with cereals, potatoes and fresh vegetables.

9.14 Beef pumpkin and vegetable stew

Reduces inflammation, improves digestion, reduces blood glucose, strengthens the muscles, tendons and bones, promotes digestion, helps to digest fat.
Cooking time approx. 1 hour
Calories p. portion: 369
4 portions
Allergens: AL

Quantity of ingredients:
Beef meat 3/4 lbs / 350g. (yes)
Pumpkin 3/4 lbs / 350g. (yes)
Leek 3/8 lbs - 6oz / 150g. (yes)
Potato 3/4 lbs / 350g. (yes)
Tomato 3/8 lbs - 6oz / 150g. (recommended)
Olive oil 2 table spoons / 25g. (yes)
Basic recipe for a vegetable soup (nutritious) 1/4 lbs - 4oz / 125g. (yes)
Salt 1 pinch / 1g. (little)
Pepper (ground) 1 pinch / 0,5g. (yes)
Peppers powder 1 teaspoon / 2g. (yes)
Ground caraway 1 pinch / 1g. (yes)
Sugar cane sugar 1 pinch / 1g. (little)
Parsley 1/2 bunch / 30g. (yes)
White bread (wheat bread) 4 slices / 80g. (little)

Cooking instructions:
Dice beef. Peel pumpkin and dice. Cut the leek into rings and dice the peeled potatoes.
Brew the tomatoes with boiling water, peel off the skin and dice.
Steam the meat in olive oil and fill with vegetable stock. Add the cleaned vegetables. Season with salt, pepper, paprika, cumin and fructose.
Stew for 30 minutes over low heat.
Season again and sprinkle with parsley and serve with white bread.

9.15 Beef salad

Strengths spleen and stomach, strengthens blood, strengthens the muscles, tendons and bones, diuretic, detoxifying, suppresses conversion of sugar into fat, lowers cholesterol, dissolves stagnation.
Cooking time approx. 10 min
Calories p. portion: 249
1 portions
Allergens: O

Quantity of ingredients:
Beef meat 1/8 lbs - 2oz / 50g. (yes)
Onion white 1/2 oz / 20g. (yes)
Peppers 1 oz / 30g. (recommended)
Cucumber (spicy cucumber) 1 oz / 30g. (recommended)
Vinegar (Apple vinegar) 2 teaspoons / 5g. (yes)
Rapeseed oil 2 teaspoons / 5g. (recommended)
Salt 1 pinch / 0,5g. (little)
Pepper (ground) 1 pinch / 0,1g. (yes)
Chives 1 table spoon / 7g. (yes)
Bread with carob kernel flour 2 slices / 50g. (yes)

Cooking instructions:
Cook the meat with the basic recipe of a beef broth and let it cool down.
Cut into 1 cm slices. Cut the onions into rings, pepper and gherkin into small cubes. Mix all ingredients.
Make the salad marinade with vinegar, oil and salt and pour over, season to taste and strain.

9.16 Beluga lentil stew with vegetables

Relieves constipation, strengthens mother milk production, detoxifying, reduces inflammation, improves blood circulation. Strengthens heart and kidney, diuretic, calms the stomach, promotes digestion.
Cooking time approx. 20 min
Calories p. portion: 201
5 portions
Allergens:

Quantity of ingredients:
Lentils 1 1/2 cups / 240g. (recommended)
Water 4-5 cups / 500g. (yes)
Carrot 3 pieces / 150g. (recommended)
Leek 1 piece / 300g. (yes)
Kohlrabi 1/2 piece / 200g. (recommended)
Tomato 2 pieces / 80g. (recommended)
Onion white 1 piece / 50g. (yes)
Bay leaf 2 leaves / 1g. (yes)
Fennel 1 piece / 250g. (recommended)
Star anise 2 pieces / 1g. (yes)
Juniper berry 6 pieces / 2g. (recommended)
Olive oil 2 table spoons / 30g. (yes)
Salt 1 pinch / 1g. (little)
Ginger fresh 1/2 teaspoon / 2g. (yes)
Black caraway 1 pinch / 1g. (yes)

Cooking instructions:
Heat oil in hot pot. Fry onions and add diced vegetables and spices, lentils (washed well) and salt. Cover with cold water (3 fingers wide) and cook for 20 minutes on a low heat.
Sprinkle with fresh herbs and black cumin
Goes well with rice!

9.17 Bitter lemon drink

Appetizing
Cooking time approx. 5 min
Calories p. portion: 130
1 portions
Allergens:

Quantity of ingredients:
Bitter Lemon 1 cup / 250g. (yes)

9.18 Blueberry puree

Bilberry is laxative. Clove dissolves stagnation. Cinnamon powder heats stomach and spleen, improves blood circulation.
Cooking time approx. 10 min
Calories p. portion: 10
1 portions
Allergens:

Quantity of ingredients:
Blueberry 1/2 oz / 20g. (yes)
Cinnamon ground 1 pinch / 0,1g. (yes)
Clove 1 piece / 1g. (yes)
Water 1 cup / 250g. (yes)

Cooking instructions:
Boil blueberries with cinnamon and clove in water for 10 minutes. Remove the cinnamon and clove. Puree. Sweet as desired.

9.19 Braised rabbit with rice and lettuce

Improves blood circulation, stimulates appetite.
Cooking time approx. 1 hour
Calories p. portion: 522
6 portions
Allergens: LMO

Quantity of ingredients:
Olive oil 2 table spoons / 20g. (yes)
Rabbit meat 1 piece (in 10-12 pieces) / 1200g. (yes)
Olive oil 2 table spoons / 20g. (yes)
Carrot 2 pieces / 180g. (recommended)
Garlic 2 cloves / 3g. (yes)
Celery sticks 1 stick / 10g. (recommended)
Onion white 1 piece / 60g. (yes)
White wine 1 1/2 cups / 250g. (little)
Water 1/2 cup / 0g. (yes)
Water 6 cups / 400g. (yes)
Rice Basmati 1 cup / 120g. (yes)
Salt 1 pinch / 1g. (little)
Lamb's lettuce 3/4 lbs / 300g. (recommended)
Olive oil 2 table spoons / 20g. (yes)
Lemon juice 1/4 piece / 8g. (yes)

Mustard 1 pinch / 1g. (yes)
Salt 1 pinch / 1g. (little)
Honey 1 pinch / 1g. (yes)

Cooking instructions:
In a heavy pan, heat the oil at low temperature. Add the rabbit parts, fry vigorously all around and then place on a plate.
Heat the oil in the pan, add the carrot, garlic, celery and onion, fry until golden brown while stirring several times and push aside.
Put the rabbit parts back into the pan, spread the vegetables over them and then pour in the wine and simmer for a few moments.
Pour in the water and heat till it boils. Put on the lid, reduce the heat supply and check in between times if there is enough liquid left. Add salt and simmer the rabbit for at least 90 minutes or until the meat is tender.
In the meantime, cook the rice in a saucepan with six times of salted water, on a low heat.
Wash the lettuce, finch and pt in a bowl. In a small bowl, mix the olive oil, lemon juice, mustard, salt and honey well and add to the salad and mix.

9.20 Broccoli cream soup

Strengthen your immune system, build and maintain healthy bones, teeth, hair and nails. Reduces blood pressure, strengthens immune system, prevents cancer, reduces radiation damage.
Cooking time approx. 30 min
Calories p. portion: 98
6 portions
Allergens: LO

Quantity of ingredients:
Olive oil 2 table spoons / 7g. (yes)
Broccoli 1,1 lbs / 500g. (recommended)
Carrot 2 pieces / 150g. (recommended)
Potato 2 pieces / 120g. (yes)
Onion white 1 piece / 50g. (yes)
Water 1 cup / 50g. (yes)
Basic recipe for a vegetable soup (nutritious) 2 cup / 500g. (yes)
White wine 1/2 cup / 125g. (little)
Sage 1 teaspoon / 2g. (yes)
Rosemary 1 teaspoon / 2g. (yes)
Pepper (ground) 1 pinch / 0,5g. (yes)
Salt 1 pinch / 1g. (little)

Cooking instructions:
Add the olive oil to the pan, add the washed and cut broccoli, diced carrots and potatoes, sauté for a short time, add the chopped onion, fill with water, enough water to cover the vegetables at least 3 finger breadths. Add bouillon, salt, add a little bit of white wine, add the seasoned sage and rosemary.
Heat till it boils and then simmer on a small fire for about 25 minutes.
Season with pepper, if necessary season with sea salt. Purée the soup.

9.21 Bulgur with tomatoes and fresh herbs

Promotes digestion, helps to digest fat, supports urination, reduces blood pressure. Stimulates digestion, supports urination.
Cooking time approx. 30 min
Calories p. portion: 205
1 portions
Allergens: A

Quantity of ingredients:
Bulgur (cereals) 1 cup / 120g. (yes)
Tomato 2 pieces / 70g. (recommended)
Rucola 2 table spoons / 16g. (recommended)
Pepper powder (hot) 1 pinch / 2g. (yes)
Olive oil 2 table spoons / 20g. (yes)
Pepper (ground) 1 pinch / 0,5g. (yes)
Salt 1 pinch / 1g. (little)
Basil 4 leaves / 2g. (yes)
Thyme 1 Twig / 3g. (yes)
Lemon juice 1/2 piece / 10g. (yes)

Cooking instructions:
Put cold water in a pot, sprinkle in Bulgur and simmer. Stir in chopped tomatoes, fresh herbs like basil, thyme, arugula, a pinch of rose paprika, lemon juice, a dash of olive oil, a little ground pepper, some salt.

Variant: add some mozzarella.

Recommendation: ideal morning meal in summer; also suitable as evening meal, especially for sleep disorders.

9.22 Carrot and rice gruel soup

Stops diarrhea, good to fight fever, strengthens immune system, reduces blood pressure.
Cooking time approx. 10 min
Calories p. portion: 101
1 portions
Allergens:

Quantity of ingredients:
Basic recipe for a rice soup (Congee) 1 cup / 120g. (yes)
Carrot 2 pieces / 100g. (recommended)
Salt 1 teaspoon / 4g. (little)

Cooking instructions:
Peel and grate carrots. Heat the rice soup (according to the basic recipe) till it boils and add the grated carrots and salt. Cook for 10 minutes.

9.23 Celery salad with lemon and olive oil

Mineral and vitamin rich, forces metabolism and dehydrating effect.
Cooking time approx. 10 min
Calories p. portion: 402
1 portions
Allergens: L

Quantity of ingredients:
Celery root 1/2 piece / 200g. (recommended)
Lemon juice 1/2 piece / 10g. (yes)
Olive oil 4 table spoons / 40g. (yes)

Cooking instructions:
Peel celeriac and cut into pieces and rub. Serve with the lemon juice and olive oil.

9.24 Chicken soup with egg yolk and parsley

Strengthens blood, strengthens bone marrow, reduces blood pressure, strengthens immune system. Parsley stimulates liver function, harmonizes liver and spleen, strengthens eyesight, detoxifying.
Cooking time approx. 10 min
Calories p. portion: 118
2 portions

Allergens: CL

Quantity of ingredients:
Basic recipe for a chicken soup (warming) 2 cup / 500g. (yes)
Chicken yolk 1 piece / 10g. (little)
Parsley 1 table spoon / 10g. (yes)

Cooking instructions:
Cook the chicken broth according to the basic recipe.
Heat broth and bubble the egg yolk. Sprinkle the chopped parsley over it and let it rest for about 2 minutes. Drink in small sips.

9.25 Colorful rice dish

Strengthens immune system, good to fight diabetes, strengthens spleen and stomach, strengthens blood, strengthens the muscles, tendons and bones, promotes digestion, helps to digest fat, supports urination, reduces blood pressure, dissolves stagnation.
Cooking time approx. 45 min
Calories p. portion: 437
3 portions
Allergens: L

Quantity of ingredients:
Olive oil 2 teaspoons / 20g. (yes)
Onion (spring onion) 1 piece / 20g. (yes)
Beef meat 1/4 lbs - 4oz / 125g. (yes)
Rice (whole grain) 3 oz / 80g. (recommended)
Basic recipe for a vegetable soup (nutritious) 1 cup / 300g. (yes)
Celery root 1/8 lbs - 2oz / 50g. (recommended)
Leek 1 piece / 100g. (yes)
Beans (green, fresh) 3/8 lbs - 6oz / 150g. (recommended)
Carrot 1 piece / 70g. (recommended)
Tomato 2 pieces / 100g. (recommended)
Salt 1 pinch / 0,5g. (little)
Pepper (ground) 1 pinch / 0,2g. (yes)
Peppers powder 1 pinch / 0,5g. (yes)
Herbs various 2 table spoons / 12g. (yes)

Cooking instructions:
Wash leek and carrots, clean and chop them. Dice the celery, slice the tomatoes.

Fry in a large, deep pan with oil, onion and minced meat.

Add brown rice and prepared vegetables (celery, leeks, beans, carrots, tomatoes). Braise briefly.

Season with salt, pepper and paprika. Add vegetable broth. Heat till it boils and cook over low heat for 20 to 30 minutes with the lid closed.

Sprinkle with fresh chopped herbs and serve.

9.26 Compote from apples

Apple (sweet) stops diarrhea, promotes digestion, appetizing, harmonizes the stomach. Warms stomach and spleen, improves blood circulation.
Cooking time approx. 10 min
Calories p. portion: 67
2 portions
Allergens:

Quantity of ingredients:
Apple (sweet) 1 piece / 220g. (recommended)
Water 1 1/2 cups / 220g. (yes)
Cinnamon ground 1 pinch / 1g. (yes)

Cooking instructions:
Cook the apples (organic) with the skin and seeds. Sprinkle with cinnamon.

9.27 Compote of pears

Pear benefits digestion, supports urination. Cocoa forces liver, strengthens the muscles, strengthens the defense. Good to fight fungi infections.
Cooking time approx. 10 min
Calories p. portion: 122
4 portions
Allergens:

Quantity of ingredients:
Water 1 cup / 280g. (yes)
Pear 4 pieces / 800g. (recommended)
Anise (Common Fennel) 1/2 teaspoon / 1g. (yes)
Vanilla pod 1 pinch / 1g. (yes)
Cocoa 1 pinch / 1g. (yes)

Cooking instructions:
Boil pears (organic - with peel), aniseed, vanilla, chili soft. Sprinkle with cocoa.

9.28 Corn coffee with cardamom

Diuretic, forcing spleen, supports urination, relaxes, reduces fat.
Cooking time approx. 5 min
Calories p. portion: 3
1 portions
Allergens:

Quantity of ingredients:
Cereal coffee 1 table spoon / 15g. (yes)
Cardamom 2 cores / 1g. (yes)
Water 1 cup / 120g. (yes)

Cooking instructions:
Boil water, coffee, sugar and cardamom. Let it set for one min before drinking.

9.29 Cream cheese substitute

Good to fight lactose intolerance. Strengthens body energy, promotes digestion, promotes weight loss. Good to fight immunodeficiency, loss of appetite, arteriosclerosis, flatulence, bladder weakness, anemia, high blood pressure, depressions, diabetes, diarrhea.
Cooking time approx. 20 min
Calories p. portion: 526
2 portions
Allergens: AE

Quantity of ingredients:
Soybean milk 4 cup / 300g. (yes)
Lemon 1 piece / 50g. (yes)
Herbs various 2 table spoons / 6g. (yes)
Whole grain bread 6 slices / 300g. (recommended)

Cooking instructions:
Heat the soy milk in a saucepan till it boils, stirring occasionally (gets burn easily!), Then allow to cool.
Squeeze out the lemon and stir gently under the cooled soy milk (approx. 80°C/176°F), let it approx. 20 min. rest or clot.
Pour chopped soy milk through a strainer lined with a dishcloth, allow liquid to drain and then squeeze out remaining liquid with the dishcloth.
Refine to taste with fresh herbs.
Serve with wholemeal bread.

9.30 Cucumber salad

Diuretic, detoxifying, suppresses conversion of sugar into fat, lowers cholesterol, prevents cancer. Cucumber cools and moistens. Dill works against flatulence, anticonvulsant in gastrointestinal discomfort.
Cooking time approx. 5 min
Calories p. portion: 27
2 portions
Allergens: O

Quantity of ingredients:
Cucumber 1 piece / 400g. (recommended)
Salt 1 pinch / 1g. (little)
Dill 1 pinch / 1g. (yes)
Vinegar (Apple vinegar) 1 table spoon / 10g. (yes)

Cooking instructions:
Cut the cucumber (do not peel the BIO) thinly and season.

9.31 Curry rice with raisins and nuts

Stops diarrhea, promotes digestion, appetizing, harmonizes the stomach, improves blood circulation, improves medication effect, stimulates appetite, detoxifies the skin, stimulates nerves, frees breathing, increases body temperature, promotes perspiration.
Cooking time approx. 30 min
Calories p. portion: 275
4 portions
Allergens: HO

Quantity of ingredients:
Sunflower oil 1 table spoon / 15g. (yes)
Onion white 1 piece / 50g. (yes)

Curry 1/2 teaspoon / 2g. (yes)
Rice wild (nature rice) 1 cup / 120g. (recommended)
Salt 1 pinch / 1g. (little)
White wine 1/2 cup / 125g. (little)
Lemon Alternatively for white wine / g. (yes)
Peppers powder 1 pinch / 1g. (yes)
Apple (sweet) 2 pieces / 300g. (recommended)
Raisins 2 table spoons / 25g. (yes)
Walnuts 2 table spoons / 25g. (recommended)
Water 6 cups / 500g. (yes)

Cooking instructions:
Heat oil in a pot; fry chopped onions until glassy; add the curry and let it
foam for a short time; then fry the raw rice for a few minutes over a
gentle heat, stirring constantly; Salt, a dash of white wine or lemon
juice, rose paprika, sweet apples chopped, raisins, chopped, roasted
nuts added; pour hot water on it until well covered; simmer until the rice
is cooked.

Goes well with: carrot and fennel vegetables, legumes with boiled
vegetables, sliced poultry with ginger and mushrooms.

9.32 Delicately spiced zucchini with tomatoes

Diuretic, promotes digestion, helps to digest fat, reduces blood
pressure, dissolves stagnation, antioxidativ, supports urination, diuretic,
warming the body from the inside, expands blood vessels.
Cooking time approx. 10 min
Calories p. portion: 203
4 portions
Allergens:

Quantity of ingredients:
Olive oil 1 table spoon / 20g. (yes)
Onion white 2 pieces / 120g. (yes)
Zucchini 4 pieces / 800g. (recommended)
Oregano dried 1 pinch / 1g. (yes)
Basil (fresh) 6-8 leaves / 3g. (yes)
Salt 1 pinch / 1g. (little)
Tomato 2 pieces / 120g. (recommended)
Rice (whole grain) 1 cup / 120g. (recommended)
Water 6 cups / 400g. (yes)
Salt 1 pinch / 1g. (little)

Cooking instructions:
In a hot pan, fry olive oil, finely chopped onions and finely chopped zucchini until half cooked. Add plenty of dried oregano. Salt and chop the tomatoes for a few minutes until the zucchini are tender but crisp. Add fresh basil as desired.

Variation: Put some sheep's cheese over the tomatoes and finish cooking with the lid closed.

Place the rice in salted water, heat till it boils and let it simmer over low heat for about 15 minutes.

9.33 Fruit juice

Stops diarrhea, promotes digestion, appetizing, harmonizes the stomach, relieves pain, detoxifying, reduces blood pressure, strengthens immune system, prevents cancer, reduces radiation damage.
Cooking time approx. 10 min
Calories p. portion: 176
2 portions
Allergens:

Quantity of ingredients:
Orange 2 pieces / 150g. (yes)
Apple (sweet) 4 pieces / 300g. (recommended)
Carrot 2 pieces / 150g. (recommended)
Honey 1 table spoon / 10g. (yes)

Cooking instructions:
Peel oranges and carrots. Cut all ingredients into cubes so that they fit into the juicer and juice. Sweet with honey.

9.34 Fruit soup with cherries, logane and lycii

Improves blood circulation, reduces inflammation, moisturizer dry skin, forcing spleen.
Cooking time approx. 10 min
Calories p. portion: 190
2 portions
Allergens:

Quantity of ingredients:
Cherry 1/4 lbs - 4oz / 100g. (recommended)
Longane 1/4 lbs - 4oz / 100g. (yes)
Lychee 1/4 lbs - 4oz / 100g. (yes)
Lemon juice 2 cup / 10g. (yes)
Cherry juice 1/2 cup / 125g. (yes)
Sugar cane sugar 2 table spoons / 20g. (little)
Rice starch 1/8 oz / 5g. (yes)
Water 1 cup / 250g. (yes)
Acerola fruit nectar or powder 1 teaspoon / 2g. (yes)

Cooking instructions:
Wash the cherries, drain and stone, peel and core the Lychee and
Logane. Boil water, sugar, fruits and lemon juice. Stir the starch until
smooth with water. Pour into the fruit with stirring, bring to the boil for 1
min and allow to cool. Stir in the acerola.

9.35 Grapefruit juice

Promotes digestion, lowers blood glucose, dries out, provides Vitamin C
Cooking time approx. 5 min
Calories p. portion: 107
1 portions
Allergens:

Quantity of ingredients:
Grapefruit (Pomelo) 1 cup / 250g. (yes)

Cooking instructions:
Juice fresh grapefruit or use organic juice.

9.36 Grilled lamb chops & sweet potato puree

Relieves weakness, strengthens lung, spleen and stomach.
Strengthens the immune system, reduces fat, improves digestion.
Cooking time approx. 45 min
Calories p. portion: 914
2 portions
Allergens: E

Quantity of ingredients:
Lamb meat 6 pieces (chops) / 300g. (yes)

Garlic 2 cloves / 3g. (yes)
Rosemary 2 table spoons / 5g. (yes)
Salt 1 pinch / 1g. (little)
Olive oil 2 table spoons / 20g. (yes)
Sweet potato 3/4 lbs / 300g. (yes)
Basil 1 table spoon / 3g. (yes)
Soybean milk 1/4 lbs - 4oz / 100g. (yes)
Basil 1 table spoon / 3g. (yes)
Salt 1 pinch / 1g. (little)
Nutmeg 1 pinch / 0,5g. (yes)
Pepper (ground) 1 pinch / 0,5g. (yes)
Chard 2 handful / 20g. (yes)
Spinach 2 handful / 20g. (yes)
Savoy cabbage / kale 2 handful / 20g. (recommended)
White cabbage 2 handful / 20g. (recommended)
Herbs various Handful / 10g. (yes)
Olive oil 2 table spoons / 20g. (yes)
Salt 1 pinch / 1g. (little)
Pepper (ground) 1 pinch / 0,5g. (yes)

Cooking instructions:
Lamb chops:
Preheat the oven grill to about 180°C/365°F and set the shelf to a
height, such that the chops are about 8 to 12 centimeters from the heat
source. Remove the most fat of the chops and place them in a fireproof
mold. Rub the meat first with garlic, then with the rosemary salt mixture
and spread a few teaspoons of olive oil over it.
Turn the lamb chops once so that they are covered with oil on both
sides, put them under the grill and grill on both sides for 5 to 7 minutes
or until the meat is well browned.

Mashed sweet potatoes:
Peel all sweet potatoes and cut into large cubes, boil gently in salted
water and strain. Leave to soak in the 100°C/212°F hot brook for a few
minutes. Remove the basil leaves. Puree sweet potatoes.
Approximately Boil 1/8 l soymilk with basil once, then strain a little and
strain and mix with the passed sweet potatoes. Season with salt,
pepper and nutmeg. Depending on the consistency of the puree, add a
little more milk.

Steamed leafy vegetables:
After the season chard, spinach, savoy cabbage, white cabbage, fresh

herbs and the mugwort in a pot with olive oil softly. Season with salt and pepper

9.37 Grilled salmon steaks with cauliflower and potatoes

Improves digestion, regenerates skin, supports urination, lowers cholesterol, supports digestion.
Cooking time approx. 30 min
Calories p. portion: 330
4 portions
Allergens: D

Quantity of ingredients:
Garlic 1 clove / 1g. (yes)
Onion (shallot) 1/2 piece / 5g. (yes)
Lemon juice 1 dash / 1g. (yes)
Salt 1 pinch / 1g. (little)
Cauliflower 1 piece / 500g. (recommended)
Olive oil 2 table spoons / 20g. (yes)
Garlic 1 clove / 1g. (yes)
Water 2/3 cup / g. (yes)
Parsley 2 table spoons / 15g. (yes)
Potato 1,1 lbs / 500g. (yes)
Salt 1 pinch / 1g. (little)
Salmon 4 pieces (steaks) / 500g. (recommended)
Lemon 1/2 piece / 2g. (yes)

Cooking instructions:
Garlic shallots mixture:
Finely squeeze the garlic, finely chop the shallots, add a dash of lemon juice and salt and stir. Mix with a little oil to a paste.

Cauliflower:
Cut the cauliflower into pieces.
Heat the oil in a heavy saucepan and fry the crushed garlic for a short time.
Add the cauliflower pieces and turn in the oil. Add a little water and cook until the cauliflower is firm. Strain the cauliflower and cook the remaining water until a thick sauce remains. Add the cauliflower and crush it roughly with a wooden spoon. Add the chopped parsley and salt.

Potatoes:
Cook the potato in a saucepan with plenty of water, strain and peel.

Salmon Steak:
Preheat the oven at about 180°C/356°F. Rub in the salmon slices with the garlic-scarlet mixture and grill as close as possible to the heat source for 4 to 8 minutes from both sides. You are done when the meat is easy to divide when you pierce with a fork.

Serve and sprinkle with lemon slices and the chopped parsley.

9.38 Grilled tofu with rice noodles, spinach and sugar snaps

Reduces flatulence. Supports urination, detoxifying. Good to fight blood circulation disorders. Strengthens gastrointestinal function, expands blood vessels, stimulates appetite. Promotes bowel movement, improves blood circulation.
Cooking time approx. 30 min
Calories p. portion: 327
4 portions
Allergens: E

Quantity of ingredients:
Sake 1/3 cup / 85g. (yes)
Sugar cane sugar 1 table spoon / 7g. (little)
Garlic 5 cloves / 7g. (yes)
Onion (spring onion) 3 pieces / 60g. (yes)
Ginger fresh 1 inch / 5g. (yes)
Rapeseed oil 2 table spoons / 20g. (recommended)
Spinach 2 handful / 30g. (yes)
Peas, green 7/8 lbs / 400g. (yes)
Water 1 table spoon / g. (yes)
Rice noodles 1 package / 250g. (yes)
Water 4 cup / g. (yes)
Basil 1 table spoon / 3g. (yes)
Soy Tofu 1,1 lbs / 500g. (yes)

Cooking instructions:
In a medium bowl mix together: Tamari souce, rice wine, sugar,

crushed garlic, spring onion, grated ginger, chopped basil and the rapeseed oil. Add the tofu and leave in the marinade for at least 1 hour. Cover the mangetout peas in a pan with a little water, lightly simmer 5 min. Add the spinach and steam again 3 min.

Cook the rice noodles according to manufacturer's instructions, drain, rinse again with warm water and drain.
Preheat the grill or oven grill, grill the tofu for 5 minutes on both sides and set aside.
Arrange the pasta on the plates, divide the vegetables all around and place the tofu over the noodles. Douse with the marinade.

9.39 Halibut with tomato and garlic sauce

Promotes digestion, helps to digest fat, supports urination, reduces blood pressure, good to fight rheumatism, flatulence, bladder weakness, anemia, high blood pressure, depressions, diabetes, diarrhea. Valuable omega-3 fatty acids.
Cooking time approx. 45 min
Calories p. portion: 319
5 portions
Allergens: D

Quantity of ingredients:
Rice variety any 1 cup / 120g. (yes)
Water 6 cups / 240g. (yes)
Salt 1 pinch / 1g. (little)
Halibut (Flatfish) 2,2 lbs / 800g. (yes)
Salt 1 pinch / 1g. (little)
Pepper (ground) 1 pinch / 0,5g. (yes)
Lemon juice 1 dash / 2g. (yes)
Bay leaf 2 pieces / 2g. (yes)
Lemon 1 piece / 30g. (yes)
Garlic 8 pieces / 10g. (yes)
Thyme dried 1 table spoon / 5g. (yes)
Olives 0,2 lbs / 75g. (yes)
Tomato 4 pieces / 200g. (recommended)
Salt 1 pinch / 1g. (little)
Pepper (ground) 1 pinch / 0,5g. (yes)

Cooking instructions:
Cook rice with salted water (1:3).

Rinse the fish under running cold water, dab with kitchen paper and rub with salt, pepper and lemon juice.
Place the fish fillets in a casserole dish with pieces of bay leaf.

Wash the lemon hot and cut into slices, peel and halve the garlic.
Sprinkle the olives and the thyme over them.
Brew the tomatoes with hot water, skin and chop.

Mix all ingredients, season with salt and pepper and distribute around the fish.

Cook everything at 200°C/392°F for about 20 minutes.
Serve with the rice.

9.40 Hearty polenta mash

Strengths spleen and stomach, promotes watering, promotes digestion, detoxifying, promotes perspiration, reduces blood lipids, stimulates, dissolves stagnation, stimulates appetite, dissolves stagnation.
Cooking time approx. 10 min
Calories p. portion: 262
2 portions
Allergens:

Quantity of ingredients:
Corn Grease (Polenta) 1 cup / 120g. (yes)
Onion (spring onion) 2 pieces / 40g. (yes)
Ginger fresh 1/2 teaspoon / 2g. (yes)
Nutmeg 1 pinch / 1g. (yes)
Salt 1 pinch / 1g. (little)
Olive oil 1 table spoon / 10g. (yes)
Turmeric (yellow root) 1 pinch / 1g. (yes)
Water 1 1/2 cups / 240g. (yes)

Cooking instructions:
Stir in the polenta in boiling water and let it swell for 7 min. Add green onion, grated ginger, turmeric, nutmeg, salt
and olive oil and wait for 3 more minutes.

9.41 Hummus (Chickpeas mash)

Relaxes breast pressure, moisturizer dry skin, helps to fight

incontinence, antioxidativ. Stimulates liver function, detoxifying, stimulates the immune system, dissolves stagnation.
Cooking time approx. 2 hours
Calories p. portion: 542
2 portions
Allergens: N

Quantity of ingredients:
Chickpeas 1 1/2 cups / 240g. (yes)
Wakame 1 teaspoon (grated) / 2g. (yes)
Ginger fresh 1/4 teaspoon / 1g. (yes)
Rosemary 1 pinch / 0,5g. (yes)
Sesame paste (Tahini) 1 table spoon / 10g. (yes)
Olive oil 2 table spoons / 20g. (yes)
Lemon juice 1 dach / 2g. (yes)
Water upon need / g. (yes)
Garlic 1 clove (scraped) / 2g. (yes)
Parsley 1 teaspoon (chopped) / 2g. (yes)
Peppers 1 pinch / 0,2g. (recommended)
Curcuma 1 pinch / 0,2g. (yes)
Coriander 1 pinch / 0,2g. (yes)
Cardamom 1 pinch / 0,2g. (yes)
Pepper (ground) 1 pinch / 0,2g. (yes)
Salt (herbal) 1/2 teaspoon / 2g. (yes)

Cooking instructions:
Soak chickpeas overnight or for at least 6 hours, pour off soaking water, boil in fresh water for about 1 to 1 ½ hours with a little seaweed and ginger, allow to cool.
Seasoning with a few splashes of lemon juice and parsley.
Add the pepper, garlic cut into small pieces or pressed, more or less coriander and cardamom powder, little chilly powder as desired, tahin and olive oil.

Puree all ingredients together. Depending on the consistency, add water. It should be a smooth paste.
Spread on cereal, crackers or toasted bread or enjoy with salad.

9.42 Italian Vegetable and Bean Soup

Promotes digestion, helps to digest fat, supports urination, reduces

blood pressure. Stimulates blood production and metabolism, reduces fat, reduces blood pressure, strengthens immune system.
Cooking time approx. 1 hour
Calories p. portion: 204
4 portions
Allergens: L

Quantity of ingredients:
Butter beans white 5/8 oz / 200g. (yes)
Onion (shallot) 1 piece / 20g. (yes)
Carrot 1 piece / 70g. (recommended)
Olive oil 2 table spoons / 20g. (yes)
Tomato 2 pieces / 80g. (recommended)
Celery root 1/4 lbs / 100g. (recommended)
White cabbage 0,2 lbs / 70g. (recommended)
Endive salad 1/8 lbs - 2oz / 50g. (yes)
Salt 1 pinch / 1g. (little)
Pepper (ground) 1 pinch / 0,2g. (yes)
Water 2 cup / 450g. (yes)

Cooking instructions:
Soak beans and cook for 1/2 hour.
Fry onions, carrots and celery in frying oil.
Add tomatoes and water and simmer for 30 minutes.
Cut white cabbage into strips. Add the cabbage and endive salad and the boiled beans, and season with salt, pepper and olive oil.

9.43 Japanese algae soup

Reduces blood pressure, strengthens immune system, prevents cancer, reduces radiation damage. Promotes digestion. Detoxifying and stimulates the immune system.
Cooking time approx. 20 min
Calories p. portion: 47
3 portions
Allergens:

Quantity of ingredients:
Wakame 1 oz / 25g. (yes)
Water 2 cup / 450g. (yes)
Onion (shallot) 1-2 pcs. / 30g. (yes)
Radish (white, green, purple-red) 1/8 lbs - 2oz / 50g. (recommended)
Carrot 2 pieces / 180g. (recommended)

Miso 2 table spoons / 20g. (yes)
Parsley 2 table spoons / 20g. (yes)
Onion (spring onion) 1 table spoon (sliced)

Cooking instructions:
Soak wakame in water for a few minutes, remove and bring the water to the boil. Add finely chopped onions and wakame, radishes and carrots, cut into thin strips, and simmer for another 10 minutes. Dissolve miso in a little cooled cooking water and add it at the end. Sprinkle with parsley and spring onions.

9.44 Kidney bean pot with lamb and sage

Relieves weakness, strengthens lung, spleen and stomach. Diuretic. Strengthens gastrointestinal function, expands blood vessels, prevents cancer, prevents diseases (in the elderly).
Cooking time approx. 1 1/2 hours
Calories p. portion: 391
4 portions
Allergens: F

Quantity of ingredients:
Soybean oil 2 table spoons / 30g. (yes)
Onion white 2 pieces / 120g. (yes)
Lamb meat 5/8 oz / 200g. (yes)
Salt 1 pinch / 0,5g. (little)
Sage 4-5 leaves / 2g. (yes)
Rosemary 1/2 teaspoon / 2g. (yes)
Thyme 1/2 teaspoon / 2g. (yes)
Kidney beans (red) 5/8 lbs - 8oz / 250g. (yes)
Water 3 cups / 750g. (yes)

Cooking instructions:
Soak kidney beans in water overnight and strain.
In a saucepan with oil, roast the onion. Dice the lamb and place in the pot. Season with salt, sage, rosemary and thyme.
Roast lamb well and cover pot. Cook over low heat and add ten-quarters of a gallon (750ml.) of cold water after 10 minutes.
Salt again.
Heat till it boils. Add beans to it.
Simmer for at least 1 hour until the beans and meat are tender.

9.45 Kudzu soup in the morning

Many vitamins and minerals. Good to fight chronic coughing, asthma, diarrhea and thirst in diabetes mellitus.
Cooking time approx. 5 min
Calories p. portion: 12
1 portions
Allergens: E

Quantity of ingredients:
Water 1 cup / 250g. (yes)
Soy sauce 1 dash / 2g. (yes)
Umeboshi paste 1 knife tip / 2g. (yes)

Cooking instructions:
Mix kudzu with cold water and heat till it boils while stirring. Once it is glassy, remove from heat and let cool. Season with Tamari and Umeboshipaste or crushed umeboshi plums

There is always the possibility to support your stomach and intestines with this recipe, taken before the right breakfast.
A morning cure for stomach and mucous membranes. Fix the base balance.

9.46 Lentil and chestnut soup with curry

Reduces blood pressure, strengthens immune system, prevents cancer, reduces radiation damage, forcing spleen, dissolves stagnation, promotes weight loss. Good to fight immunodeficiency, loss of appetite, flatulence, high blood pressure, depressions, diabetes, diarrhea.
Cooking time approx. 45 min
Calories p. portion: 176
4 portions
Allergens: LO

Quantity of ingredients:
Lentils red 3/8 lbs - 6oz / 150g. (yes)
Chestnuts 3/8 lbs - 6oz / 150g. (yes)
Olive oil 1 table spoon / 10g. (yes)
Curry 2 teaspoons / 8g. (yes)
Turmeric (yellow root) 1 teaspoon / 2g. (yes)
Basic recipe for a vegetable soup (nutritious) 2 cup / 500g. (yes)
White wine 1/2 cup / 125g. (little)
Salt (herbal) 1 pinch / 1g. (yes)

Anise (Common Fennel) 1 pinch / 1g. (yes)
Cardamom 1 pinch / 0,5g. (yes)
Cardamom 1 pinch / 1g. (yes)
Parsley 2 table spoons / 6g. (yes)

Cooking instructions:
Add the olive oil to a pan, sauté the chestnuts, sprinkle with the curry, add the lentils and season with vegetable stock, add a little white wine, mix in the curcuma, simmer for about 20 minutes (until the chestnuts are tender).
Then puree the soup.
Taste with a pinch of anise, cardamom and herbal salt. At the end, sprinkle finely chopped parsley over it.

9.47 Lettuce with fresh cheese

The bitter substances have diuretic effect and promote the blood circulation in the digestive area. Mustard improves thyroid function, relieves rheumatism symptoms.
Cooking time approx. 5 min
Calories p. portion: 802
1 portions
Allergens: AFM

Quantity of ingredients:
Leaf salads (bitter) 2 portions / 60g. (recommended)
Fresh cheese from soya 3/8 lbs - 6oz / 150g. (yes)
Mustard 1 knife tip / 1g. (yes)
Lemon juice 1 dash / 3g. (yes)
Salt 1 pinch / 1g. (little)
Pepper (ground) 1 pinch / 0,5g. (yes)
Herbs various 2 teaspoons / 4g. (yes)
Black caraway 1 pinch / 1g. (yes)
Whole grain bread 2 slices / 40g. (recommended)

Cooking instructions:
Wash lettuce and finely pluck.
Mix 150 ml cream cheese, splashes of mustard, splashes of lemon juice, 1 clove of garlic, chopped fresh herbs, pinch of pepper and crushed black cumin and pour over. Serve with wholemeal bread.

9.48 Marinated turkey with cashew nuts from the wok

Strengthens blood, strengthens bone marrow, for the drainage of the body overweight and high blood pressure. Promotes digestion, helps to digest fat, supports urination, reduces blood pressure.
Cooking time approx. 30 min
Calories p. portion: 319
4 portions
Allergens: ELNO

Quantity of ingredients:
Turkey breast meat 3/4 lbs / 300g. (recommended)
Sake until covered / g. (yes)
Sesame oil 2 table spoons / 30g. (recommended)
Ginger fresh 1/2 teaspoon / 2g. (yes)
Salt 1 pinch / 0,5g. (little)
Lemon 1/2 piece / 15g. (yes)
Red wine 1/2 cup / 125g. (little)
Sugar cane sugar 1 pinch / 1g. (little)
Onion (spring onion) 4 pieces / 80g. (yes)
Tomato 2 pieces / 100g. (recommended)
Basic recipe for a chicken soup (warming) 1 cup / 120g. (yes)
Cashews 2 table spoons / 16g. (yes)
Soy sauce 1 dash / 2g. (yes)
Rice Basmati 1 cup / 120g. (yes)
Water 6 cups / 400g. (yes)
Salt 1 pinch / 0,5g. (little)

Cooking instructions:
Preparation: cover sliced turkey meat with rice wine; marinate overnight or for a few hours.
Then: strain and drain well; heat sesame oil in a hot wok; fry finely chopped ginger; sauté the meat for a short time; add the marinade; add salt, lemon juice, red wine or rose paprika; let the meat soak in the sauce for 2 - 3 minutes; then exhaust it; add some sugar to the sauce in the wok; add a few spring onions (the white parts), a pinch of salt, chopped tomatoes, 1 cup of chicken broth; simmer so that the onions are still crisp.
Roasted cashews, add the cashews and the meat to the sauce and heat; season with soy sauce; stir in the green of the chopped green onions.
Boil the rice with the water, salt and cook for about 20 minutes.

9.49 Miso soup with tofu

Vitamins, minerals and secondary plant active ingredients, invigorating, detoxifying, strengthens immune system, promotes digestion, forcing spleen, containing enzymes, reduces flatulence, alginic acid detoxifies the bowel, dissolves stagnation.
Cooking time approx. 5 min
Calories p. portion: 51
3 portions
Allergens: E

Quantity of ingredients:
Wakame 1 piece / 5g. (yes)
Miso 3-4 table spoons / 30g. (yes)
Soy Tofu 1/8 lbs - 2oz / 50g. (yes)
Water 2 cup / 500g. (yes)
Soy sauce 1 dash / 3g. (yes)
Onion (spring onion) 1/2 teaspoon / 6g. (yes)

Cooking instructions:
Boil soybean seedlings, wakame algae and diced tofu for 5 minutes. Put the miso paste in the soup plate and slowly pour over the soup. Season with Tamari sauce. Sprinkle with cutted spring onion.

9.50 Pear compote

Promotes digestion, supports urination.
Cooking time approx. 20 min
Calories p. portion: 100
3 portions
Allergens:

Quantity of ingredients:
Water 1 1/2 cups / 240g. (yes)
Pear 4 / 500g. (recommended)

Cooking instructions:
Halve organic pears. Cores and skin can be used. Pear in the pot and add water. Simmer for up to 20 minutes until pears are tender.

9.51 Polenta with peach

Relieves fatigue, forcing spleen, diuretic, strengthens the defense, good to fight fungi infections, lets urine and bile juice flow, prevents the aging process, strengthens brain cells.
Cooking time approx. 20 min
Calories p. portion: 197
3 portions
Allergens:

Quantity of ingredients:
Water 1 1/2 cups / 240g. (yes)
Corn Grease (Polenta) 1 cup / 120g. (yes)
Peaches 2-3 pieces / 400g. (recommended)
Vanilla pod 1 pinch / 1g. (yes)
Cinnamon ground 1 pinch / 1g. (yes)

Cooking instructions:
Pour the polenta into a pan of hot water with constant stirring until the polenta has the desired consistency. Pull the polenta from the fire and let it soak for 10 minutes.

Wash fresh peaches and cut into quarters. Pour into the finished polenta the peaches, add the vanilla and add Chili to taste, stir and let it go for 3 minutes.

Winter varieties: Pickled fruit, pear, apples

9.52 Porcino mushroom-smoked tofu on toast bread

Good to fight loss of appetite, flatulence, improves digestion, improves thyroid function.
Do not eat together with spinach!
Cooking time approx. 1 hour
Calories p. portion: 169
2 portions
Allergens: AEMO

Quantity of ingredients:
Boletus mushroom 3/8 lbs - 6oz / 150g. (yes)
Soy Tofu smoked 5/8 oz / 200g. (yes)
Olive oil 1/2 teaspoon / 5g. (yes)
Pickle 1 table spoon / 10g. (yes)
Nutmeg 1 pinch / 1g. (yes)

Salt 1 pinch / 1g. (little)
Miso paste (soy bean paste) 1/4 cup / 50g. (yes)
Lemon peel 1 teaspoon / 2g. (yes)
Mustard Dijon 2 teaspoons / 6g. (yes)
Pepper (ground) 1 pinch / 0,5g. (yes)
Toast bread (whole grain) 6 slices / 30g. (yes)

Cooking instructions:
Use fresh or dried mushrooms. Soak the dried porcini mushrooms in
250 ml of hot water for 1 hour. Drain the mushrooms and cut small.
Collect the soaking water and pour it through a fine sieve.
Heat olive oil lightly in a small, coated pan. Add the mushrooms, lightly
salt, season with nutmeg and sauté briefly while stirring, add 6
tablespoons of soaking water, simmer gently until the liquid has
evaporated.

Mix smoked tofu, the mushrooms, chopped pickle, soy cream, grated
lemon peel and Dijon mustard with the cutter or the blender to a smooth
spread.

Season the spread with salt and pepper. Serve on the toast bread
slices.

9.53 Potato with dandelion salad

Promotes spleen, reduces inflammation, improves digestion,
regenerates skin, supports urinating, lowers cholesterol, detoxifying,
reduces inflammation, forcing spleen and digestive system, detoxifying,
dissolves stagnation.
Cooking time approx. 25 min
Calories p. portion: 162
2 portions
Allergens:

Quantity of ingredients:
Potato 5/8 lbs - 8oz / 250g. (yes)
Onion white 1/2 piece / 20g. (yes)
Sunflower oil 1 table spoon / 10g. (yes)
Dandelion (young plants) 1/4 lbs - 4oz / 125g. (yes)
Salt 1 pinch / 1g. (little)
Pepper white (ground) 1 pinch / 0,5g. (yes)

Cooking instructions:
Cook the potatoes in salted water and cut into thin slices. Finely chop the onion. Now season the potatoes with oil, salt and pepper and add the dandelion and mix.

9.54 Potato-basil soup

Reduces inflammation, improves digestion, supports urination, lowers cholesterol, reduces blood pressure, strengthens immune system, prevents cancer, reduces radiation damage, antioxidativ, dissolves stagnation.
Cooking time approx. 25 min
Calories p. portion: 96
4 portions
Allergens: L

Quantity of ingredients:
Water 2 cups / 450g. (yes)
Potato 4 pieces / 200g. (yes)
Carrot 2 pieces / 100g. (recommended)
Celery root 1 piece / 500g. (recommended)
Pepper (ground) 1 pinch / 0,5g. (yes)
Ground 1 pinch / 1g. (yes)
Garlic 1 clove / 3g. (yes)
Salt 1 pinch / 1g. (little)
Lemon 1 teaspoon / 3g. (yes)
Basil (fresh) 1 Bunch / 50g. (yes)
Peppers powder 1 pinch / 1g. (yes)
Sugar cane sugar 1 pinch / 1g. (little)
Olive oil 1 table spoon / 10g. (yes)

Cooking instructions:
Peeled and chopped 4 medium potatoes in a pot of hot water and 2 chopped medium carrots, a piece of celery root, a pinch of pepper, a pinch of ground cumin, crushed a small clove of garlic, a pinch of salt, 1 teaspoon of lemon juice, simmer until the Vegetables is soft.

Add 1 bunch finely chopped basil into one half of the soup and puree everything; stir in the other half of the basil; with rose paprika, a pinch of whole cane sugar, 1 tablespoon of olive oil or butter, freshly ground pepper, salt to taste.

9.55 Pumpkin curry

Promotes digestion and sweating, Dissolves stagnation, strengthens lungs and spleen, diuretic, reduces blood glucose, forcing spleen and digestive system, detoxifying, strengthens the muscles and bones.
Cooking time approx. 20 min
Calories p. portion: 193
3 portions
Allergens:

Quantity of ingredients:
Pumpkin 3/4 lbs / 300g. (yes)
Olive oil 2 table spoons / 30g. (yes)
Coriander 1 pinch / 1g. (yes)
Pepper (ground) 1 pinch / 0,5g. (yes)
Curry 1 pinch / 1g. (yes)
Water 1/4 cup / 50g. (yes)
Salt 1 pinch / 1g. (little)
Parsley 1 table spoon / 7g. (yes)
Cardamom 1 pinch / 1g. (yes)
Turmeric (yellow root) 1 pinch / 1g. (yes)
Rice (whole grain) 1/2 cup / 60g. (recommended)
Water 3 cups / 300g. (yes)
Salt 1 pinch / 1g. (little)

Cooking instructions:
Heat olive oil in pan. Steam the pumpkin cut in cubes, season with cilantro, pepper and curry, simmer with a little water, salt with sea salt, add chopped parsley with cardamom and turmeric, simmer on a small fire for about 10 minutes, depending on the pumpkin, the pumpkin should still be firm.
Place the rice in salted water, bring to the boil and let it simmer over low heat for about 15 minutes.

9.56 Pumpkin soup

Promotes digestion, forcing spleen and stomach, reduces blood pressure, strengthens immune system, prevents cancer, reduces radiation damage, improves digestion, regenerates skin, lowers cholesterol, reduces blood glucose, protects liver.
Cooking time approx. 1 hour
Calories p. portion: 105
3 portions
Allergens:

Quantity of ingredients:
Pumpkin 3/4 lbs / 300g. (yes)
Carrot 2 pieces / 100g. (recommended)
Potato 2 pieces / 120g. (yes)
Olive oil 1 table spoon / 10g. (yes)
Onion white 1 piece / 50g. (yes)
Water 1 cup / 120g. (yes)
Parsley 1 table spoon / 7g. (yes)
Anise (Common Fennel) 1 pinch / 1g. (yes)
Salt 1 pinch / 1g. (little)

Cooking instructions:
Add the olive oil to the pan, add the diced pumpkin, diced carrots and potatoes. Roast them shortly, add the finely chopped onion, fill with water, add enough water to cover the vegetables at least 3 finger-widths. Boil at low heat.
Season with sea salt, add small cutted parsley, a pinch of anise (little). Allow to simmer for about 35 minutes. Then purée the soup and add some water, depending on the consistency of the soup.

9.57 Puréed banana

Eat 2 times a day, regulates gastrointestinal function
Cooking time approx. 7 min
Calories p. portion: 144
1 portions
Allergens:

Quantity of ingredients:
Banana 1 piece / 150g. (yes)

Cooking instructions:
Mix the banana with the fork or purée with a blender. Leave to brown for at least 5 minutes.

9.58 Rhubarb and apple jelly

Antioxidants, lots of vitamin C, laxative, relieves pain, detoxifying, warms stomach and spleen, improves blood circulation.
Cooking time approx. 15 min
Calories p. portion: 180
2 portions
Allergens:

Quantity of ingredients:
Rhubarb 5/8 oz / 200g. (recommended)
Apple juice (natural cloudy) 1 cup / 300g. (yes)
Corn starch 1 oz / 30g. (yes)
Honey 1/2 oz / 20g. (yes)
Vanilla sugar natural 1 pinch / 0,5g. (yes)
Cinnamon ground 1 pinch / 0,5g. (yes)
Peppermint 2 leaves / 2g. (yes)

Cooking instructions:
Add the cornstarch to a 1/2 cup apple juice.
Simmer the rhubarb in 1 cup of water for 10 min.
Add the remaining apple juice and the cornstarch, stir, heat till it boils again.
Sweet with honey and season with vanilla and cinnamon. Spread the mixture on dessert bowls and garnish with mint.

9.59 Rice congee with honey pear and black sesame

Promotes digestion, supports urination, good to fight blood circulation disorders, thromboses, risk of embolism, high blood pressure, a headache, heart attack and stroke.
Cooking time approx. 10 min - 3 hours
Calories p. portion: 158
2 portions
Allergens: N

Quantity of ingredients:
Basic recipe for a rice soup (Congee) 1 1/2 cups / 240g. (yes)
Pear 2 pieces / 300g. (recommended)
Sesame, black 1 teaspoon / 3g. (yes)

Cooking instructions:
Cook rice congee according to basic recipe.
Fill pot with 3 cm of water and heat till it boils. Quarter the pears (with the skin and seeds) and simmer them covered with black sesame for 10 minutes. Mix with the rice.

9.60 Rice congee with mung beans

Good to fight blood circulation disorders, diarrhea, antipyretic, high blood pressure, a headache. To drain the body overweight and high blood pressure. Relieves excessive thirst, supports urination, reduces blood lipids, relieves allergies.
Cooking time approx. 2 hours
Calories p. portion: 424
2 portions
Allergens:

Quantity of ingredients:
Basic recipe for a rice soup (Congee) 4 cups / 500g. (yes)
Mung bean 1/2 cup / 50g. (yes)
Herbs various 2 table spoons / 8g. (yes)
Rapeseed oil 2 table spoons / 20g. (recommended)

Cooking instructions:
Soak the mung beans the day before and strain. Cook the rice according to the basic recipe and cook the mung beans with the rice. Finally, add fresh herbs and a dash of high-quality cold-pressed oil.

9.61 Rice noodle soup with shiitake mushrooms

Very light and powerful. Strengthens the immune system.
Cooking time approx. 20 min
Calories p. portion: 66
2 portions
Allergens: L

Quantity of ingredients:
Rice noodles 2 handful / 20g. (yes)
Shiitake, dried 4-6 pieces / 5g. (yes)
Basic recipe for a vegetable soup (nutritious) 1 1/2 cups / 240g. (yes)
Chinese cabbage 1 cup / 60g. (recommended)
Lovage 1 teaspoon / 3g. (yes)
Miso 2 table spoons / 18g. (yes)

Cooking instructions:
Soak rice noodles and shiitake mushrooms separately in cold water. Heat the vegetable broth and add the soaked shiitake mushrooms cut into strips and simmer gently. Cut Chinese cabbage into noodles, add

lovage green and rice noodles and let it steep for a while. Before serving, stir in Miso dissolved in a little cooled water.
Recommendation: Suitable at the beginning of each meal, also for breakfast

9.62 Rice pesto with pine nuts

Worming spleen and stomach, harmonizes the intestine.
Cooking time approx. 30 min
Calories p. portion: 274
4 portions
Allergens:

Quantity of ingredients:
Rice variety any 1 1/2 cups / 200g. (yes)
Water 4 cup / 950g. (yes)
Garlic 4 big cloves / 8g. (yes)
Basil Handful / 15g. (yes)
Pine nuts 2 table spoons / 30g. (yes)
Olive oil 2 table spoons / 20g. (yes)

Cooking instructions:
Boil the rice with 1 liter of water. Finely crush the peeled garlic in a mortar or puree with a hand mixer. Add finely crushed basil leaves, then purée the pine nuts a little coarser. Lastly, gradually add the oil until a thick paste forms.
Mix the pesto sauce with the finished rice.

9.63 Roasted barley patties

Improves digestion, lowers cholesterol, good to fight diarrhea, ulceration, joint pain, stomach problems. Promotes spleen and liver, reduces blood pressure, strengthens immune system, prevents cancer, reduces radiation damage, stimulates liver function.
Cooking time approx. 1 1/2 hours
Calories p. portion: 398
3 portions
Allergens: ACN

Quantity of ingredients:
Water 1 1/2 cups / 250g. (yes)
Barley grouts 1 cup / 120g. (yes)
Potato 1 piece / 140g. (yes)
Carrot 1 piece / 120g. (recommended)

Champignon 2-3 pieces / 25g. (yes)
Chicken egg 1 piece / 55g. (yes)
Onion white 1 piece / 50g. (yes)
Ginger fresh 1/2 teaspoon / 1g. (yes)
Pepper (ground) 1 pinch / 0,5g. (yes)
Salt 1 pinch / 1g. (little)
Lemon 1/2 piece / 15g. (yes)
Parsley 2 table spoons / 15g. (yes)
Peppers powder 1 pinch / 1g. (yes)
Sesame oil 2 table spoons / 50g. (recommended)
Bread roll 1 piece / 35g. (little)

Cooking instructions:
Preparation:
Place 2 large cups of hot water in a saucepan; add 1 large cup of barley porridge; simmer for 2 minutes while stirring; then let it swell for 20 minutes on the switched off stove; take down and let cool.

Cook in boiling water 1 large potato, chopped and cut.

Soak 1 roll in hot water and squeeze well.

Then: Mix the barley groats and crushed the potato. Add 1 grated carrot, 2 - 3 chopped mushrooms, 1 egg, 1 finely chopped onion, 1/2 teaspoon grated ginger, a pinch of pepper, a pinch of salt, a little lemon juice, chopped parsley, plenty of rose paprika; knead well and form patties; heat sesame oil in a hot pan; fry the patties for about 15 minutes over a gentle heat; turn at half time.

Also fits well: lettuce, soybean vegetables.

9.64 Rucola salad with tomatoes

Promotes digestion, helps to digest fat, supports urination, reduces blood pressure, stimulates digestion, strengthens the muscles, antioxidativ, helps to fight gastritis, flatulence and heartburn.
Cooking time approx. 10 min
Calories p. portion: 129
1 portions
Allergens: O

Quantity of ingredients:
Olive oil 1 table spoon / 10g. (yes)
Pepper (ground) 1 pinch / 0,2g. (yes)
Salt 1 pinch / 0,3g. (little)
Vinegar (Apple vinegar) 1 dash / 1g. (yes)
Tomato 4 pieces / 200g. (recommended)
Rucola 2 handful / 30g. (recommended)

Cooking instructions:
In a salad bowl stir in olive oil, freshly ground pepper, salt, vinegar and diced tomatoes; plenty of finely shredded rucola leaves.
Variants: Cut shiitake mushrooms into fine strips: Fry one half in a little butter and mix with the other half of raw shiitake under the salad. In place of shiitake mushrooms can be used.
Serve with: toasted bread, polenta.

9.65 Salmon on tomato-spinach

Promotes bowel movement, improves blood circulation, forcing spleen and bowel, strengthens blood, reduces inflammation, improves digestion, regenerates skin, supports urination, lowers cholesterol, promotes sweating, dissolves stagnation.
Cooking time approx. 1 hour
Calories p. portion: 365
6 portions
Allergens: D

Quantity of ingredients:
Potato 1,1 lbs / 500g. (yes)
Salt 1 pinch / 1g. (little)
Salmon 1,3 lbs / 600g. (recommended)
Rapeseed oil 2 teaspoons / 24g. (recommended)
Tomato 1/4 lbs - 4oz / 100g. (recommended)
Spinach 1,5 lbs / 700g. (yes)
Salt 1 pinch / 1g. (little)
Pine nuts 4 table spoons / 40g. (yes)
Leek 1/4 lbs - 4oz / 120g. (yes)
Olive oil 4 table spoons / 40g. (yes)
Salt 1 pinch / 1g. (little)
Pepper white (ground) 1 pinch / 0,5g. (yes)

Cooking instructions:
Peel the potato and cut into cubes, cook in salted water.
Cut the salmon into portions and fry slowly and evenly in a frying pan from both sides, seasoned with salt and pepper, then add the pine nuts and lightly roast.
Blanch spinach in salted water.
Lightly sweat the finely chopped leek with a little rapeseed oil, add the blanched spinach and heat evenly.
Just before serving, add the halved cocktail tomatoes to the spinach and season the vegetables well with salt and pepper.
Arrange the spinach and leek tomato bed with the potatoes, add the salmon and sprinkle with the salted pine nuts.
Drizzle with a little olive oil and serve the dish.

9.66 Scrambled eggs with leaf salad olives and tomatoes

Calms nerves and stomach, relieves fatigue, regulates gastrointestinal function, promotes digestion, stimulates liver function, detoxifying, helps to digest fat, supports urination, reduces blood pressure.
Cooking time approx. 10 min
Calories p. portion: 419
1 portions
Allergens: C

Quantity of ingredients:
Chicken egg 2-3 pieces / 180g. (yes)
Olive oil 1 table spoon / 10g. (yes)
Salt 1 pinch / 1g. (little)
Pepper (ground) 1 pinch / 0,5g. (yes)
Olives 6 pieces / 10g. (yes)
Tomato 1 piece / 50g. (recommended)
Lettuce 2 leaves / 5g. (recommended)
Turmeric (yellow root) 1 pinch / 1g. (yes)
Parsley 1/2 teaspoon / 5g. (yes)
Basil (fresh) 2-3 leaves / 2g. (yes)

Cooking instructions:
Heat olive oil in the pan. Cut the tomato into a slice. Pluck salad into small pieces. Briefly fry tomatoes, lettuce and olives. Meanwhile mix eggs with salt and spices with a fork.
Pour the egg and spices into the pan. Stir with a wooden spoon until it reaches the desired consistency.

Spices and herbs: turmeric, parsley, basil, black cumin
Variation: zucchini, rocket

9.67 Sliced lamb with rosemary potatoes

Improves digestion, regenerates skin, supports urination, lowers cholesterol, reduces blood pressure, strengthens immune system. Strengthens gastrointestinal function, expands blood vessels.
Cooking time approx. 1 hour
Calories p. portion: 461
4 portions
Allergens: LO

Quantity of ingredients:
Lamb meat 7/8 lbs - 1 lbs / 500g. (yes)
Olive oil 2 table spoons / 20g. (yes)
Onion white 1 piece / 50g. (yes)
Garlic 1 clove / 2g. (yes)
Nutmeg 1 pinch / 0,2g. (yes)
Carrot 3 pieces / 150g. (recommended)
Celery root 1/4 tuber / 120g. (recommended)
Rosemary 1 Twig / 3g. (yes)
Savory 1 teaspoon / 2g. (recommended)
Parsley 1 table spoon / 8g. (yes)
Pepper powder (hot) 1 pinch / 2g. (yes)
Red wine 1/2 cup / 125g. (little)
Salt (herbal) 1 pinch / 1g. (yes)
Lemon juice 1/2 piece / 15g. (yes)
Cranberry 1 table spoon / 10g. (recommended)
Potato 6 pieces / 400g. (yes)

Cooking instructions:
Cut the lamb into strips, cut the carrots and celery into small cubes. Heat the olive oil in a pan, fry the lamb in it, add the cut onions and garlic, salt with herbal salt, a little water, parsley, deglaze with red wine, season with paprika and small cut rosemary, mugwort, savory, carrots and celery, turn the heat back on small Simmer for about 35 minutes. Season with pepper and nutmeg, if necessary still salt, add a little lemon juice, season with paprika, cranberries.
Cut the potatoes in half, the length of, spread a little olive oil on the cut surface, salt, sprinkle 2-3 rosemary needles on each half potato, place the potatoes on the baking sheet and bake in a preheated oven for approx. 25 minutes at 190°C/374°F.

9.68 Spinach with Tahini

Promotes bowel movement, improves blood circulation, forcing spleen and bowel, improves pancreatic function. Improves digestion, regenerates skin, supports urination, lowers cholesterol. Gentle laxative.
Cooking time approx. 20 min
Calories p. portion: 150
4 portions
Allergens: N

Quantity of ingredients:
Potato 1,1 lbs / 500g. (yes)
Salt 1 pinch / 0,2g. (little)
Water 1 cup / 25g. (yes)
Spinach 2,2 lbs / 800g. (yes)
Sesame paste (Tahini) 2 table spoons / 20g. (yes)

Cooking instructions:
Cook potatoes and peel. Heat water. Blanch spinach. Shake off water and let it dry and stir with sesame.

9.69 Sweet potato pancakes with basil pesto

Strengthens the immune system, reduces fat, Improves digestion, calms nerves and stomach, dissolves stones, improves blood circulation, strengthens the muscles, antioxidativ.
Cooking time approx. 30 min
Calories p. portion: 625
3 portions
Allergens: ACH

Quantity of ingredients:
Sweet potato 4 pieces / 500g. (yes)
Onion read 1/2 piece / 30g. (yes)
Basil 1 table spoon / 10g. (yes)
Chicken egg 2 pieces / 140g. (yes)
Spelled wholemeal flour 3 oz / 80g. (yes)
Salt 1 pinch / 0,5g. (little)
Olive oil 1/4 cup / 20g. (yes)
Salt 1 teaspoon (coarse) / 3g. (little)
Basil Handful / 15g. (yes)
Parsley Handful / 15g. (yes)
Garlic 2 cloves / 3g. (yes)

Walnuts 1/8 lbs - 2oz / 60g. (recommended)
Olive oil 2 table spoons / 20g. (yes)

Cooking instructions:
Sweet Potato Buffer: Wash the sweet potato thoroughly, but do not peel, and grate into a large bowl. Add onion, basil, egg and flour, mix well and sprinkle with salt. The mixture can be formed into buffers. Bake in a preheated tube on a baking tray coated with oil for 4 to 5 minutes on both sides.

Basil Pesto: Add the salt, chopped basil and parsley and crushed garlic in a small bowl and crush (if available, use the mortar). Add the grated walnuts. While stirring, add enough olive oil until the desired consistency is achieved.

9.70 Thick pea soup

Supports urination, detoxifying, dissolves stagnation, improves blood circulation, strengthens liver and kidney, strengthens immune system.
Cooking time approx. 2-3 hours
Calories p. portion: 123
3 portions
Allergens: AN

Quantity of ingredients:
Peas, green 3/8 lbs - 6oz / 150g. (yes)
Water 2 1/4 cups / 550g. (yes)
Sesame oil 1 table spoon / 20g. (recommended)
Onion white 1/2 piece / 25g. (yes)
Ginger fresh 1/2 teaspoon / 1g. (yes)
Ground 1/2 teaspoon / 1g. (yes)
Oat meal 1 table spoon / 15g. (yes)
Salt 1 pinch / 1g. (little)
Parsley 1 stem / 2g. (yes)

Cooking instructions:
Soak dried peas before cooking. Sauté sesame oil, onion, a little oatmeal, ginger and cumin in a hot pot; add the peas and simmer for 2-3 hours; add salt at the end and purée with a blender; garnish with parsley.

9.71 Tomato soup

Promotes digestion, helps to digest fat, supports urination, reduces blood pressure, dissolves stagnation. Contains unsaturated fatty acids, is antioxidativ.
Cooking time approx. 10 min
Calories p. portion: 100
2 portions
Allergens:

Quantity of ingredients:
Olive oil 1 table spoon / 15g. (yes)
Onion white 1 piece / 60g. (yes)
Basil (fresh) 1 teaspoon / 2g. (yes)
Cinnamon ground 1 pinch / 1g. (yes)
Pepper (ground) 1 pinch / 0,5g. (yes)
Salt 1 pinch / 1g. (little)
Tomato 6 pieces / 250g. (recommended)
Water 5/8 lbs - 8oz / 250g. (yes)
Peppers powder 1 pinch / 1g. (yes)

Cooking instructions:
Roast the onion in a pot. Salt and spices. Briefly roast. Put washed and quartered tomatoes in the pan. Stir and sauté briefly. Add a quart of water and heat till it boils. Cook for a quarter of an hour and puree.

9.72 Vegetable bowl with tofu and curry on rice

Reduces flatulence, supports digestion. Contains ideal herbal mucus, which provides regeneration of the small and large intestinal flora. Reduces blood pressure, strengthens immune system.
Cooking time approx. 30 min
Calories p. portion: 162
6 portions
Allergens: E

Quantity of ingredients:
Olive oil 2 table spoons / 20g. (yes)
Garlic 2 cloves / 3g. (yes)
Onion white 1 piece / 60g. (yes)
Curry 2 table spoons / 16g. (yes)
Water 2 cup / 500g. (yes)
Turnips 2 pieces / 50g. (recommended)
Pumpkin 1 piece / 400g. (yes)

Carrot 1 piece / 100g. (recommended)
Parsnip 1 piece / 150g. (yes)
Potato 1 piece / 70g. (yes)
Sweet potato 1 piece / 70g. (yes)
Cauliflower 1/4 piece / 250g. (recommended)
Broccoli 1/2 piece / 250g. (recommended)
Okra 12 pieces / 200g. (yes)
Soy Tofu 1 piece / 250g. (yes)
Basil 2 table spoons / 12g. (yes)
Salt 1 pinch / 0,5g. (little)

Cooking instructions:
Heat the oil at medium temperature in a large, heavy casserole, add the garlic and onion and sauté with constant stirring. Sprinkle curry powder over it, fry gently for about 5 minutes and make sure that the garlic and curry do not burn. Add the water and heat till it boils. Gradually peel all vegetables, dice and add, starting with the varieties that need the longest cooking time. Once the water has boiled again, reduce the heat and simmer the vegetables for about 15 minutes. When it is almost soft. Add the cauliflower and broccoli florets and the okra and cook the stew for another 10 to 15 minutes. Add the tofu during the last 5 minutes. Cook the brown rice at the same time: Sprinkle the rice in a medium saucepan with water, salt and cover for about 20 minutes. cook on a low heat. Take from the fire and another 10 min. to let go.
Arrange the stew over the brown rice and sprinkle with basil.

9.73 Vegetable juice

Promotes digestion, helps to digest fat, supports urination, reduces blood pressure, strengthens immune system, prevents cancer, reduces radiation damage, forcing spleen, is stimulating.
Cooking time approx. 15 min
Calories p. portion: 64
1 portions
Allergens: L

Quantity of ingredients:
Celery root 1/2 oz / 20g. (recommended)
Carrot 1/4 lbs - 4oz / 100g. (recommended)
Tomato 1/4 lbs - 4oz / 100g. (recommended)
Garlic 1 piece / 2g. (yes)
Salt 1 teaspoon / 2g. (little)
Acerola fruit nectar or powder 1/2 teaspoon / 1g. (yes)

Cooking instructions:
Peel all ingredients and use the juicer to make a drink. Stir in the acerola.

9.74 Vegetable rice

Forcing spleen, dissolves stagnation, promotes weight loss. Good to fight immunodeficiency, loss of appetite, flatulence, high blood pressure, strengthens kidney and bladder. Diuretic, warming the body from the inside, regulates internal organs functions.
Cooking time approx. 30 min
Calories p. portion: 304
3 portions
Allergens: L

Quantity of ingredients:
Broccoli 1/8 lbs - 2oz / 50g. (recommended)
Carrot 1/8 lbs - 2oz / 50g. (recommended)
Kohlrabi 1/8 lbs - 2oz / 50g. (recommended)
Cauliflower 1 oz / 30g. (recommended)
Peas 1/2 oz / 20g. (yes)
Margarine 1 teaspoon / 4g. (yes)
Rice (whole grain) 5/8 oz / 200g. (recommended)
Basic recipe for a vegetable soup (nutritious) 7/8 lbs / 400g. (yes)
Parsley 1/2 oz / 20g. (yes)
Pepper (ground) 1 pinch / 0,2g. (yes)

Cooking instructions:
Cut the broccoli, carrots and kohlrabi into small cubes, divide the cauliflower into small florets. Heat the margarine in a pan or saucepan, sauté the vegetables. Then add the rice, top up with the vegetable stock and leave to soak for 15-20 minutes.

In the meantime finely chop the parsley. After cooking, season the rice with freshly ground pepper and parsley.

9.75 Vegetarian vegetable-oatmeal-potatoes mash

Improves digestion, regenerates skin, supports urination, lowers cholesterol, supports urination, relieves constipation, strengthens mother milk production.
Cooking time approx. 25 min
Calories p. portion: 91

2 portions
Allergens: A

Quantity of ingredients:
Carrot (Early Carrot) 1 oz / 30g. (recommended)
Parsnip 1 oz / 30g. (yes)
Zucchini 1 oz / 30g. (recommended)
Fennel 1/2 oz / 10g. (recommended)
Potato 1/8 lbs - 2oz / 50g. (yes)
Water 1/2 oz / 20g. (yes)
Oat flakes (whole grain) 1/2 oz / 10g. (recommended)
Orange juice 1 oz / 30g. (yes)
Rapeseed oil 1/4 oz / 8g. (recommended)

Cooking instructions:
Wash the vegetables and potatoes, dice and fry in a little water. Add water and oatmeal, puree everything and finally add the oil. Note: This porridge replaces the vegetable-potato-meat porridge when meat is to be dispensed with in the infant's diet. Since meat is the best food source for iron, a vegetarian diet must pay particular attention to a sufficient supply of iron.

9.76 Yellow lentil soup

Strengthens heart and kidney, diuretic, promotes spleen, calms the stomach, promotes digestion, strengthens immune system, prevents cancer, reduces radiation damage, stimulates liver function, antioxidativ.
Cooking time approx. 20 min
Calories p. portion: 155
7 portions
Allergens: A

Quantity of ingredients:
Lentils yellow 1 lbs / 500g. (yes)
Carrot 2 pieces / 150g. (recommended)
Kohlrabi 1 piece / 300g. (recommended)
Onion white 1 piece / 50g. (yes)
Parsley 1/2 bunch / 100g. (yes)
Turmeric (yellow root) 1 pinch / 1g. (yes)
Cardamom 1 pinch / 1g. (yes)
Salt 1 pinch / 1g. (little)
Olive oil 1 table spoon / 10g. (yes)

Water 4 cup / 1000g. (yes)
Lemon juice 1/2 piece / 15g. (yes)
White bread (wheat bread) 7 slices / 140g. (little)

Cooking instructions:
Wash lenses well in a colander. Heat oil in a pot. Add finely chopped onion, sliced carrots, diced kohlrabi and spices, sauté and salt. Add the lentils and cover with water and simmer for 20 minutes. Add water as needed and season with salt. Sprinkle with fresh parsley or fresh green cilantro and drizzle with lemon juice.
Here you can also use red lenses. (same cooking time).
Serve with white bread.

10 Effects of food

10.1 Use ingredients: recommendable

Acai powder
Apple (sour)
Apple (sweet)
Apple puree
Asparagus (green or white)
Beans (green, fresh)
Bitter Herb liqueur
Blackberry's
Borage
Broccoli
Brussels sprouts
Carrot
Carrot (Early Carrot)
Carrot juice without sugar
Cauliflower
Celery root
Celery sticks
Cherry
Cherry (sour)
Chicory
Chinese cabbage
Cod
Corn germ oil
Cranberry
Cranberry juice
Cream 10% coffee cream
Cucumber
Cucumber (bitter)
Cucumber (spicy cucumber)
Currant (black)
Currant (red)
Currant (white)

Fennel
Fish pieces mixed (fresh water)
Fox nut, gorgon nut, makhana
Gourd
Herbal tea mix
Herring
Hibiscus
Juniper berry
Kohlrabi
Kudzu
Lamb's lettuce
Lamb's lettuce
Leaf salads (bitter)
Lentils
Lettuce
Lily bulbs
Linseed oil
Mackerel
Manioc flour
Mascarpone cheese
Mediterranean fish (cod, plaice, haddock, sea eel, mackerel)
Muesli
Noodles (whole grain) with egg
Oat flakes (whole grain)
Oat fusion (baby food)
Peaches
Peaches (canned)
Pear
Peppers
Plaice
Plum

Plums
Radicchio
Radish
Radish (white, green, purple-red)
Radish horseradish
Rapeseed oil
Raspberry
Red beet
Red cabbage
Rhubarb
Rice (whole grain)
Rice mash
Rice wild (nature rice)
Rose hip
Rose hip tea
Rosefish
Rucola
Rye wholemeal bread
Salmon
Savory
Savoy cabbage / kale
Sesame oil

Soya Cuisine (soy cream)
Soybeans
Strawberries
Tomato
Trout
Tuna
Turkey breast meat
Turnip
Turnips
Vegetable juice
Walnuts
Watermelon
Wax gourd
Wheat bran
Wheat flour whole grain
Wheat germ oil
Wheat/Rye/Gray-black bread with yeast
White cabbage
Whole grain bread
Wholemeal flour
Wild herbs
Zucchini

10.2 Use ingredients: yes

Acerola fruit nectar or powder
Adzuki beans
Agar agar (kelp)
Agave nectar
Agrimony
Almond
Almond marzipan
Almond milk
Almond puree
Aloe juice
Amaranth
Amaranth Pops
Anchovy / Sardine
Angelica root
Anise (Common Fennel)
Apple juice (natural cloudy)
Apricot
Apricot dried
Apricot jam
Apricot nectar
Apricots
Apricots juice
Arrowroot
Artichoke
Aubergine
Avocado
Baking powder
Balm
Bamboo shoots

Banana
Banana (cooking banana)
Banchatee (green tea)
barberry
Barley
Barley flour
Barley grass powder
Barley grouts
Barley malt
Barley not peeled
Basic recipe for a beef soup
Basic recipe for a beef soup (warming)
Basic recipe for a chicken soup (warming)
Basic recipe for a duck soup
Basic recipe for a fish soup
Basic recipe for a rice soup (Congee)
Basic recipe for a vegetable soup (nutritious)
Basil
Basil (fresh)
Batavia
Bay leaf
Bean oil
Bearberry leaf
Beef bone marrow
Beef fillet
Beef heart
Beef heart (calf)

Beef lungs (calf)
Beef meat
Beef meat (calf)
Beef meatbones
Beef Oxtail pieces
Beef soup meat
Beef stomach
Berries of the season
Berry juice
Bitter Lemon
Bitter orange peel
Black beans
Black caraway
Black fungus mushroom
Black tea
Blackberry dried (unripe fruit)
Blackberry jam
Blackberry leaves
Black-eyed peas
Blackthorn (Sloe)
Blue mallow tee
Blueberry
Blueberry dried
Blueberry jam
Blueberry juice
Bocksdorn fruits (Fructus Lycii, Goji, goji berry dried
Boletus mushroom
Borage oil
Boxhorn clover seeds
Brazil nuts
Bread with carob kernel flour
Breadcrumbs (wheat bread, bread roll)
Broad beans (thick beans)
Buckbean
Buckwheat
Buckwheat (roasted) Kasha
Buckwheat whole grain
Bulgur (cereals)
Burdock root tea
Bush beans
Butter beans white
Calamari
Cantaloupe
Capers in olive oil
Carambola (Star fruit)
Cardamom
Carob flour, St. john's bread
Carp
Cashews
Caviar
Cereal coffee
Chamomile
Chamomile tea

Champignon
Channa-Dal
Chanterelle
Chard
Chenpi (chinese tangerine bowl)
Cherry compote
Cherry juice
Chervil
Chervil dried
Chestnut puree
Chestnuts
Chicken Blood
Chicken egg
Chicken egg white
Chicken heart
Chicken meat
Chicken stomach
Chickpeas
Chickweed
Chili (pod or ground)
Chinese pearl barley
Chives
Chlorella (fresh water)
Chrysanthemum blossom tea
Cinnamon ground
Cinnamon sticks
Clementine
Clementines
Clove
Cocoa
Coconut flakes
Coconut grated
Coconut meat
Coconut milk
Codfish
Coffee
Coix (seeds) YiYi Ren
Cola drink (low calorie)
Compote (fruits of the season)
Cooking oil
Coriander
Coriander (fresh)
Corn
Corn (fast polenta)
Corn (roasted)
Corn flour
Corn Grease (Polenta)
Corn silk tea
Corn starch
Couscous
Crab
Cranberries
Cranberry
Cranberry jam

Creamer
Cress
Crispbread
Crucian
Cumin (Caraway seed)
Curcuma
Currant jam (black)
Currant jam (red)
Currant juice (black)
Currants (black)
Currants (red)
Curry
Curry paste red
Daisy
Dandelion (young plants)
Dandelion juice
Dandelionroots tea
Dashi
Dates dried
Dates red
Deer meat
Deer meat
Deer's Bones
Deer's kidneys
Dill
Duck (heart)
Duck (slaughtered)
Ducks egg
Dulse (seaweed)
Dyer's broom herb
Eel
Eel smoked
Elderberries
Elderberry blossom tee
Endive salad
Evening primrose oil
Fennel seeds ground
Fennel tea
Fenugreek (Trigonella foenum-graecum)
Fig
Fig dried
Fish sauce
Flounder
Flower pollen
French beans
Fresh cheese from soya
Freshwater crab
Freshwater fish
Fructose (glucose)
Fruit mix juice
Fruit tea
Gail plum
Galangal

Garam Masala powder
Garlic
Gelatin white
Gelee Royal
Gentian root
Gentian root tea
Ginger fresh
Ginger oil
Ginger powder
Ginkgo fruit
Ginseng
Ginseng root
Goat
Goat and sheep's blood
Goat and sheep's brain
Goat and sheep's stomach
Goose
Goose blood
Goose egg
Goose fat
Goose parts
Gooseberry
Grape juice red
Grape juice white
Grapefruit (Pomelo)
Grapefruit dried peel
Grapefruit juice
Grapes red
Grapes white
Grapeseed oil
Grass carp
Green spelt
Green tea
Greengage
Ground
Ground caraway
Guava
Halibut (Flatfish)
Hawthorn
Hazelnuts
Herbs bitter
Herbs of Provence
Herbs various
Herbs wild
Hibiscus tea
Hijiki
Hokkaido pumpkin
Honey
Hop
Horehound leaves
Horse meat
Hyssop
Iceberg lettuce
Jasmine blossoms tee

Jellyfish
Kaki plum
Kalmus
Kidney beans (red)
King Solomon's-seal
Kiwi
Kombu seaweed (Saccharina japonica)
Kukicha tea
Kumquats
Ladyfingers
Lamb bones
Lamb meat
Lamb shoulder
Lavender blossoms
Leek
Lemon
Lemon Balm (dried)
Lemon Balm (fresh)
Lemon juice
Lemon peel
Lemongrass
Lentils black
Lentils red
Lentils yellow
Licorice root tea
Lima beans
Lime
Lime blossom tea
Linseed
Linseed (crushed)
Liver smoothing tea
Lobster
Longane
Loquate / Japanese medlar
Lotus roots
Lotus seeds
Lovage
Lovage seeds
Luo Han Guo fruit
Lychee
Lychee in Preserved
Lye roll
Mallow (Malva sylvestris) blossom tea
Malt
Mango
Mango juice
Maple syrup
Margarine
Margarine (diet)
Marjoram
Medlar
Millet
Millet flakes
Mineral water

Mirabelle plum
Miso
Miso black (fermented)
Miso paste (soy bean paste)
Mixed Pickles
Morel (black, dried)
Morel, dried
Mu Erh Mushroom
Mulberry fruit
Mulled Wine Spice
Mullet
Multi-grain bread (gray bread)
Mung bean
Mung bean sprouting
Mussels
Mustard
Mustard Dijon
Mustard medium hot
Mustard seeds
Mustard sweet
Mutton
Mutton
Nasturtium (nose-twister or nose-tweaker)
Nectarine
Nettles
Noodles (wheat) with egg
Noodles (wheat, lasagne) with egg
Noodles (wheat, ribbon noodles) with egg
Noodles (wheat, spaghetti) with egg
Nori, purple seaweed, red algae
Nutmeg
Oat
Oat flakes roasted
Oat flour
Oat meal
Oat milk
Octopus
Octopus
Okra
Olive oil
Olives
Olives green
Onion (shallot)
Onion (spring onion)
Onion read
Onion white
Orange
Orange blossom
Orange dried peel
Orange grated peel
Orange jam
Orange juice

Orange peel
Oregano dried
Oregano fresh
Oyster mushroom
Oyster shell powder
Oysters
Palm oil
Papaya
Parmesan
Parsley
Parsley root
Parsnip
Passion blossoms tea
Passion fruit
Peanut butter
Peanut oil
Peanuts
Pear juice
Pearl barley
Pearl barley
Peas
Peas, green
Pepper (ground)
Pepper Cayenne
Pepper powder (hot)
Pepper white (ground)
Peppercorns
Peppermint
Peppermint tea
Pepperoni
Pepperoni, red, pitted, halved
Pepperoni, yellow, pitted, halved
Peppers (rose peppers)
Peppers (sweet)
Peppers powder
Perch
Pheasant
Pickle
Pig blood
Pigeon
Pigeon egg
Pimento
Pine nuts
Pineapple
Pineapple (from a can)
Pineapple juice without sugar
Pinto beans speckled
Pistachios
Plum dried
Pomegranate
Poppy
Pork Bacon
Pork brain
Pork fat (lard)

Pork ham
Pork ham cooked
Pork ham smoked
Pork knuckle
Pork lung
Pork marrow bones
Pork meat
Pork sausage (Bratwurst)
Pork skin
Pork stomach
Pork/beef sausage (smoked)
Pork's intestine
Potato
Potato (mealy)
Potato flour
Prickly pear
Psyllium seed
Pudding powder vanilla
Puff pastry
Pumpernickel (dark bread)
Pumpkin
Pumpkin seed oil
Pumpkin seeds
Quail
Quail egg
Quince
Quinoa
Rabbit
Rabbit (wild)
Rabbit liver
Rabbit meat
Radish black
Radish leaves
Raisins
Raspberry dried (immature)
Raspberry jam
Raspberry leaf tea
Red berry (without sugar)
Reishi mushroom
Ribworttea
Rice (fragrance)
Rice (Gaoliang / Sorghum)
Rice Basmati
Rice black
Rice flour
Rice long grain rice
Rice malt
Rice noodles
Rice red
Rice round grain
Rice starch
Rice sticky
Rice sweet
Rice variety any

Romaine lettuce / lettuce salad
Rose blossom tea
Rose leaf tea
Rosemary
Rusk
Rye
Rye flour
Safflower (Dyer's thistle / Hong Hua)
Saffron
Sage
Sago (cereals)
Sake
Salsify
Salt (herbal)
Sauerkraut (cutted cabbage fermented)
Sea buckthorn
Sea cucumber
Seacrab
Sesame oil roasted
Sesame paste (Tahini)
Sesame, black
Sesame, white
Shark
Shiitake, dried
Shrimp
Shrimps
Slug
Sorrel
Sour cherries
Sourdough
Soy flour
Soy noodles
Soy sauce
Soy Tofu
Soy Tofu smoked
Soybean milk
Soybean oil
Soybeans, black
Soybeans, blacks, fermented
Soybeans, yellow
Spelled (Dark) bread
Spelled flakes
Spelled grain
Spelled semolina
Spelled wholemeal flour
Spinach
Spiny lobsters
Spurdog (spiny dogfish, Schillerlocken)
St. Benedict's thistle, blessed thistle,
holy thistle, spotted thistle
Star anise
Stevia (candyleaf, sweetleaf)
Strawberry jam
Strawberry Juice

Sugar fructose - fruit sugar
Sugar glucose - grapes sugar
Sugar Milk Sugar
Sugar substitute (sweetener)
Sunflower oil
Sunflower seeds
Sweet potato
Tabasco
Tangerine
Tarragon (Estragon)
Tea mixture uric acid lowering
Thistle oil
Thyme
Thyme dried
Toast bread (whole grain)
Tomato dried
Tomato juice
Tomato paste
Tomato puree
Tonic Water
Topinambur
Trout (smoked)
Truffle
Tsampa (roasted barley flour)
Turkey ham
Turmeric (yellow root)
Umeboshi paste
Umeboshi plums (Japanese apricots)
Valerian
Vanilla
Vanilla pod
Vanilla powder
Vanilla sugar natural
Vinegar (Apple vinegar)
Vinegar (Red wine vinegar)
Vinegar Aceto Balsamico
Vinegar Aceto Balsamico white
Wakame
Walnut oil
Walnuts roasted
Water
Water hot
Wheat
Wheat bulgur
Wheat flakes
Wheat flatbread/pita bread
Wheat flour
Wheat semolina
Wheat semolina for children
Wheatgrass juice
Wheatgrass powder
White beans
Whitefish
Wild boar meat

Wild garlic (garlic spinach)
Wild strawberries
Wormwood herb
Yam root, yam root tuber
Yarrow

Yarrow tea
Yeast
Yew nut
Yogi tea

10.3 Use ingredients: little

Beef kidney
Beef liver
Beer (alcohol-free)
Beer (alcohol-reduced)
Beer (Pils)
Beer (Top-fermented German dark beer)
Bitter liqueur
Bread roll
Brown ale
Campari
Chicken liver
Chicken yolk
Chocolate
Chocolate (Diabetic)
Clarified butter
Coconut fat
Cola drink
Edam cheese
Emmental cheese
Fernet Branca (herbal bitter liqueur)
Fish innards
Fish remains
Ginseng liqueur
Goat and sheep's liver
Gouda cheese
Honey wine (Met)
Lamb kidneys
Lamb liver
Lychee liqueur
Martini

Mayonnaise 50%
Mayonnaise 80%
Peanut (roasted)
Pork heart
Pork kidneys
Pork Lard
Pork liver
Prosecco
Red wine
Rum
Salt
Sherry (whine)
Spirit
Sugar - icing sugar
Sugar brown
Sugar candy white
Sugar cane sugar
Sugar molasses
Sugar palm sugar
Sugar white
Wheat beer
White bread (baguette)
White bread (pretzel sticks)
White bread (roll)
White bread (wheat bread)
White breadcrumbs
White dumpling bread (wheat bread cut into chunks)
White wine
Wormwood

10.4 Do not use contra-acting foods

Brie cheese
Butter (half fat)
Butter organic
Buttermilk
Camembert
Cottage cheese
Cow's milk (1.5% fat)
Cow's milk (whole milk 3.5% fat)
Cream (30% fat)
Cream sour 10%
Cream sour 20%

Cream sour 30%
Cream, sweet 30%
Créme fraiche cheese
Curd cheese 20%
Curd cheese 40%
Feta cheese
Feta cheese
Fresh cheese
Fresh cheese with herbs
Goat and sheep's milk
Goat cheese

Gorgonzola
Kefir
Mare's milk
Mold cheese
Mozzarella
Processed cheese 12%
processed cheese 30%
Sheep's milk
Sheep's milk yoghurt

Skim milk powder
Sour cream 15% fat
Sour milk
Sour milk cheese 20%
Supplementary nutrition
Whey
Yoghurt vanilla
Yogurt (natural, 1.5% fat)
Yogurt (natural, 3.5% fat)

11 Herbs and their effects

11.1 Basil

It has a beneficial effect on flatulence and nausea, relaxing and soothing. Good to fight emphysema, bronchitis, whooping cough, high blood pressure, headache, mouth odor, warts, hiccup, gout, migraine.

11.2 Mugwort

Reduces bleeding, alleviates pain. In the kitchen, mugwort is used as a spice for fat food. Since it contains many bitter substances, it boosts fat burning and promotes digestion.

11.3 Savory

Stomach-strengthening, soothing and appetizing. Ideal for prevent colds, strengthens the immune system. In case of incontinence or nocturnal wetting (not for children), put the beans in liquor for libido.

11.4 Dill

The medicinal and spice herb has an antispasmodic effect and stimulates gastric juice production. Good to fight flatulence. Antispasmodic for gastrointestinal discomfort.

11.5 Chervil dried

Forces urination, detoxifying, blood-purifying and blood-pressure-reducing effects.

11.6 Coriander

The essential oils are appetizing, digestive, cramping and soothing in stomach and intestinal disorders.

11.7 Herbs various

Appetizing, lots of trace elements and vitamins

11.8 Chives

Bactericide, prevents cancer, strengthens gastric juice production, promotes digestion and blood circulation, promotes growth, triggers stagnation.

11.9 Lovage

Stimulates digestion, reduces pain. Extracts of the root are used to flush out urinary tract infections and prevent kidney gravel.

11.10 Lily bulbs

Calms nerves, good to fight scaly skin. The onions and the petals are added to ointments in the Orient, which can heal muscles and tendons. White lily (astringent).

11.11 Dandelion (young plants)

Detoxifies, relieves inflammation. Regulates digestion, helps with rheumatism, releases kidney stones, leaves pimples and chronic skin disorders disappear.

11.12 Oregano dried

It has an anti-digestive, calming and nerve-strengthening effect, helps to fight cramping stomach and intestinal disorders. The ingredient Carvacrol has an anti-inflammatory effect.

11.13 Parsley

Stimulates liver function, detoxifies. Forces urinating. Relieves flatulence. Digestive and menstrual stimulating, birth-accelerating, memory-enhancing, blood-purifying, skin-smoothing.

11.14 Peppermint

Relaxes, frees the lungs and the nose (inhale), regulates the cycle. Stimulates bile flow and bile production, antispasmodic in gastrointestinal disorders, antimicrobial and antiviral.

11.15 Rosemary

Promotes digestion, relieves bloating, strengthens lung, spleen and kidney. Affects the circulation and nerves. Appetizing. Baths help to fight circulatory disorders as well as with gout and rheumatism.

11.16 Sage

Good to fight yeast infections. The leaves have a digestive effect and are used in greasy foods. Antiperspirant effect. Helps to relieve coughing attacks. Dries out (TCM).

11.17 Black caraway

Detoxifying, immunoregulatory. In addition, the oil should stimulate the formation of bone marrow cells and generally protect body cells from viruses.

11.18 Thyme dried

Disinfecting. It stimulates the blood circulation, increases the appetite and helps to digest fat meat better. Strengthens lungs and spleen (TCM).

11.19 King Solomon's-seal

Used to repair wounds or damaged tissue. Good to fight dry cough, earlier also tuberculosis and dysentery, as well as diarrhea and hemorrhoids.

11.20 Yam root, yam root tuber

Solves cramps (in the gastrointestinal tract). Digestive through increased bile production. Anti-inflammatory in rheumatic diseases.
Mucolytic agent for coughing. Relief of menopausal symptoms.

12 Basics of Nutrition

The basic principles of nutrition described herein are general recommendations. They are not aimed at a specific form of therapy. Recommendations concerning a therapy have priority.

12.1 Nutrition

Regular meals in a relaxed atmosphere. A warm breakfast is considered a good start into the day.
The main meals ought to be taken for lunch – supper in the early evening. Pay attention to feeling hungry or sated: don't eat too much nor remain hungry is the rule
Prepare the meals freshly from natural, regional products. Frozen, heat-conserved, industrially prepared or foodstuffs cooked in the microwave oven are rejected.
Choice of foodstuffs according to the season: more cooling food in summer, more warming food in winter.
Eat cooked food at least twice a day. Food and drinks ought to be lukewarm, never ice-cold or hot.
Raw vegetables, briefly cooked vegetables, freshly squeezed juices and mineral water are not recommended. Milk and dairy products are only included in the diet if they don't cause problems.
Don't use therapeutic recipes over a longer period without consulting your doctor or therapist.

Varied food
Enjoy the diversity of foodstuffs. Characteristics of a balanced nutrition are variety, suitable combination and a balanced quantity of rich and low energy foodstuffs (on one hand avoiding undersupply with essential nutrients and on the other hand to take to many undesirable substances).

A lot of Cereal Products - and Potatoes
Bread, pasta, rice, cereal flakes (best wholemeal) as well as potatoes contain almost no fat, but many vitamins, mineral nutrients, trace elements, roughage and secondary plant substances. These foodstuffs ought to be taken with low-fat side dishes.

Vegetables and Fruit – „Take Five" every day ...
5 portions of vegetables and fruit a day, as fresh as possible, briefly cooked, or maybe one portion as a juice – ideal as a side dish to every meal as well as snack between meals: Thus a lot of vitamins, mineral nutrients as well as roughage and secondary plant substances

Daily milk and dairy products
Milk and Dairy Products every Day, once or twice per Week Fish;
meat, sausages as well as eggs moderately. These foodstuffs contain
valuable nutrients like calcium in the milk, iodine selenium and omega-3
fat acids in saltwater fish. Meat is favorable due to its high content of
disposable iron and the vitamins B1, B6 and B12. Quantities of 300 – 600
g meat and sausage per week are sufficient. Prefer low-fat products,
especially in meat- and dairy products.

Low-fat and fatty Foodstuffs
Fat supplies us with essential fat acids and fatty foodstuffs contain also
fat-soluble vitamins. Fat is high in energy; therefore much fat in the food
may cause overweight, possibly also cancer. Too many saturated fat
acids may further a tendency for cardio-vascular diseases in the long
term. Prefer vegetable oils and fats (e.g. rapeseed-, olive-, soya-oils and
solid fats produced therefrom). Beware of invisible fat in meat- and dairy
products, pastry and sweets as well as in fast-food and convenience
foods. 70 – 90 g fat per day is sufficient.

Moderately Sugar and Salt
Take sugar and foods/drinks containing various kinds of sugar (e.g.
glucose syrup) only occasionally. Use herbs and spices as well as a little
salt creatively. Prefer salt containing iodine.

Plenty of Liquids
Water is absolutely essential. Drink 1-2 l liquids every day. Prefer water
(with or without gas) and other low-calorie drinks. Alcoholic drinks should
not be taken.

Tasty Dishes, carefully cooked
Cook the meals with as low temperatures and as short as possible, using
little water and fat – this preserves the original taste, keeps the nutrients
intact and prevents the production of harmful compounds.

Take time and enjoy the food
Take your Time and enjoy your Food
Eating consciously helps to eat right. The eye enjoys food, too. It's fun,
invites to enjoy varied dishes and stimulates the feeling of satiety.

Watch your Weight and stay in Motion
A balanced diet and a lot of exercise and sport (30 – 60 min/day) are a
healthy combination. The right weight furthers well-being and health.
Thermals, directional effectiveness, digestive power

There are various criteria for judging the effectiveness of herbs and foodstuffs.

The use of certain herbs and ingredients is based on observations of the effects on the body which these foodstuffs, herbs and spices show after having eaten them. The medical science has developed following system: Every ingredient or herb has a directional effectiveness. Furthermore, there are herbs which have a special effect on certain organs.

The basic condition for a healthy metabolism is to obtain sufficient energy from food and that the digestive process doesn't use too much energy. An easily digestible meal makes content and sated, doesn't cause flatulence and fatigue after the meal. The perfect spices increase the healthiness of our meals. Very often, just small doses of herbs and spices will suffice. They are not used to make us sated, but to help our digestive organs to digest the food.

12.2 Recipes

The recipes list the ingredients to be used and the cooking instructions show how the dish is prepared. The list of ingredients shows the concerned quantities as well as the relevance for the therapy. If you find „less than mentioned", try to comply or find an alternative from the „list of recommended foodstuffs". Mostly it shall result just in a small change of taste when you simply avoid this ingredient.

Mild cooking methods: boiling, stewing, poaching, steaming
Strong cooking methods: barbecuing, roasting, frying, smoking
Balanced cooking methods: deep-frying, baking brick
Deep-freezing and warming in the microwave oven should be avoided (denaturalization).

12.3 Foodstuffs

Foodstuffs have an effect on body and soul like medicinal herbs, only a very much milder one. Dietary advice is mainly based on regional foodstuffs. The knowledge about the effects of each foodstuff and the knowledge, when which foodstuff shall be used, is based on the orthodoschool of medicine. Use ecologic-organic products, if possible. As everything should be cooked for a long time due to a better digestability and very rarely eaten raw, the food agrees with everyone.

The classification of the foodstuffs according to their effect on the body is the basis in order to achieve a harmonious status of health.

Dietary advisors do not recommend certain foodstuffs for everyone. The individual diet is tailor-made for the individual constitution.

Buy only fresh and ripe fruit and vegetables. You ought to leave unripe fruit and vegetables and such with brown spots and wilted leaves behind in the market. In this case take deep-frozen goods (never ready-to-serve dishes!). Fruit and vegetables are deep-frozen immediately after harvesting and often contain more vitamins and minerals than the goods from the vegetable shelf. Whereas conserved or tinned goods contain very much less biological substances. Also, salt, sugar and others are mostly added to the latter. Never leave the foodstuffs in the water after washing them to avoid that many vital substances get drowned. Clean salads, fruit and vegetables immediately before serving.

Please make sure of the hygienic processing of foodstuffs. Clean your salads, fruit and vegetables carefully. When cooking with meat, prepare all ingredients first and then process the meat products. Clean the worktop and tools very carefully. Wooden surfaces ought to be treated with a mild disinfectant regularly in order to reduce germination.

Store fruit and vegetables separately, if possible. Harvested fruit and vegetables are still alive and emit e.g. ethylene gas, which makes other products ripen and age faster. Keep meat and fish in the closed packaging or store them in the fridge in closed containers.

12.4 Herbs

There are some basic rules for storing medicinal herbs. On principle, herbs must be protected from direct sunlight, humidity and heat.

Containers for the storage of herbs may be glasses, ceramic jars and even plastic containers. However, plastic is a rather unsuitable material and should only be a short-term solution. In case of glass containers, use a dark material.

Medicinal herbs cannot be kept for any long period. The shelf life of herbs is limited. However, it can be prolonged with suitable storage. The place should be dark, rather cool and absolutely dry. A wooden medicine cabinet, placed not directly next to a source of heat, would be ideal. Never buy large quantities of herbs so as not to have to throw them away. Label the container with the name of the herb and the date of harvesting or processing.

13 Other dietic-books

The following syndromes of dietetics, TCM or for a therapy supplement for cancer are available.

Dietetics

E001. Nutrition of the infant - baby food
E002. Nutrition during lactation
E003. Nutrition in old age
E004. Nutrition of children and adolescents
E005. Nutrition of athletes
E006. Light weight
E007. Pregnancy
E008. Full food

Protein and electrolyte - kidneys
E009. (hemodialysis) dialysis treatment
E010. Acute renal failure
E011. Chronic renal insufficiency
E012. Nephrotic syndrome
E013. Kidney stones (nephrolithiasis)

Gastrointestinal tract - pancreas
E014. Acute pancreatitis (inflammation of the pancreas)
E015. Chronic pancreatitis (inflammation of the pancreas)

Gastrointestinal tract - small intestine and large intestine
E016. Acute obstipation (constipation)
E017. Chronic obstipation (constipation)
E018. Colon irritabile
E019. Diverticulitis
E020. Acquired lactose intolerance (lactose malabsorption)
E021. Fructose malabsorption
E022. Glutensensitive enteropathy (celiac disease)
E023. Colectomy
E024. Short Bowel Syndrome

Gastrointestinal tract - liver, gallbladder, bile ducts
E025. Acute and chronic hepatitis (inflammation of the liver)
E026. Cholelithiasis (bile stones)
E027. fatty liver
E028. cirrhosis

Gastrointestinal tract - Stomach and duodenal intestine
E029. Acute gastritis
E030. Chronic gastritis
E031. Stomach bleeding
E032. Ulcus ventriculi and duodenal ulcer
E033. Condition after gastric surgery

Gastrointestinal tract - oral cavity and esophagus
E034. Stomatitis
E035. Esophageal carcinoma (esophageal cancer)
E036. Refluosophagitis (heartburn)

Special diseases
E037. Phenylketonuria (PKU)
E038. Rheumatic joint diseases

Metabolism
E039. Obesity (overweight)
E040. Diabetes mellitus
E041. Eating disorders (underweight)

Fat metabolism
E042. Hypercholesterolaemia (increased cholesterol level)
E043. Hepatic Encephalopathy

Heart and circulation
E044. Arteriosclerosis (arterial calcification)
E045. Heart insufficiency
E046. Hypertension
E047. Hyperuricaemia and gout

Changed nutrient requirements
E048. In case of fever
E049. For malignant diseases
E050. After burns
E051. Radiation and chemotherapy

CANCER
E100. Pancreatic cancer
E101. Bladder cancer
E102. Blood cancer (leukemia)
E103. Breast cancer
E104. Colorectal cancer
E105. Gastric cancer
E106. Kidney cancer
E107. Esophageal cancer

TCM
E200. Bladder - moisture heat in the bladder
E201. Bladder - moisture and cold in the bladder
E202. Bladder - emptiness and cold in the bladder
E203. Large intestine - external cold affects the large intestine
E204. Large intestine - moisture heat in the large intestine
E205. Large intestine - heat blocks the intestine II acute
E206. Large intestine - dryness of the colon
E207. Large intestine - Yang deficiency (cold)
E208. Heart - Blood insufficiency
E209. Heart - Blood stagnation
E210. Heart - Fire
E211. Heart - Hot mucus clogs the heart pores

E212. Heart - Cold mucus clogs the heart pores
E213. Heart - Qi deficiency
E214. Heart - Yang deficiency
E215. Heart - Yin deficiency
E216. Liver - Ascending Liver Yang
E217. Liver - Blood deficiency
E218. Liver - Blood stagnation
E219. Liver - Moisture heat in liver and gall bladder
E220. Liver - Fire
E221. Liver - Gall bladder Qi-Empty
E222. Liver - Cold in the liver meridian
E223. Liver - Qi stagnation
E224. Liver - Wind
E225. Liver - Wind with ascending liver Yang
E226. Liver - Wind with blood anemic
E227. Liver - Wind with extreme heat
E228. Lung - Qi deficiency
E229. Lung - Mucus-moisture in the lungs
E230. Lung - Mucus-heat in the lungs
E231. Lung - Mucus-cold in the lungs
E232. Lung - Dryness of the lungs
E233. Lung - Wind-heat attacks the lungs
E234. Lung - Wind-cold affects the lungs
E235. Lung - Yin deficiency
E236. Stomach - Bloodstagnation
E237. Stomach - Fire
E238. Stomach - Cold with liquid
E239. Stomach - Nutrition stagnation
E240. Stomach - Qi deficiency
E241. Stomach - Rebellious Qi
E242. Stomach - Yin Emptiness
E243. Spleen - Heat and moisture attack the spleen
E244. Spleen - Coldness and moisture affects the spleen
E245. Spleen - Qi deficiency
E246. Spleen - Qi deficiency + Declining spleen Qi
E247. Spleen - Qi deficiency + spleen does not control the blood
E248. Spleen - Yang deficiency
E249. Kidney - Heart and kidney no longer communicate
E250. Kidney - Jing deficiency
E251. Kidney - Kidneys cannot receive the Qi
E252. Kidney - Qi is not stable
E253. Kidney - Yang deficiency
E254. Kidney - Yin deficiency

For further information visit di-book.com.